Spray Paint Paper Crafts

Spray Paint Paper Crafts

Creative Fun with Krylon

A LARK/CHAPELLE BOOK

A Division of Sterling Publishing Co., Inc.
New York

A Lark/Chapelle Book

Chapelle, Ltd., Inc.
P.O. Box 9255, Ogden, UT 84409
(801) 621-2777 o (801) 621-2788 Fax
e-mail: chapelle@chapelleltd.com
Web site: www.chapelleltd.com

Created and produced by Red Lips 4 Courage Communications, Inc.
www.redlips4courage.com
Eileen Cannon Paulin
President
Catherine Risling
Director of Editorial

Library of Congress Cataloging-in-Publication Data

Currier, Sharon.
 Spray painted paper crafts : creative fun with krylon / by Sharon
Currier.
   p. cm.
Includes index.
ISBN 1-57990-995-7 (hardcover)
1. Paper work. 2. Painting--Technique. I. Title.
TT870.C83 2006
745.54--dc22
                              2006011400

10 9 8 7 6 5 4 3 2 1

First Edition

Published by Lark Books, A Division of
Sterling Publishing Co., Inc.
387 Park Avenue South, New York, N.Y. 10016

Distributed in Canada by Sterling Publishing, c/o Canadian Manda
Group, 165 Dufferin Street, Toronto, Ontario, Canada M6K 3H6

Distributed in the United Kingdom by GMC Distribution Services,
Castle Place, 166 High Street, Lewes, East Sussex, England BN7 1XU

Distributed in Australia by Capricorn Link (Australia) Pty Ltd.,
P.O. Box 704, Windsor, NSW 2756 Australia

Manufactured in China

ISBN 13: 978-1-57990-995-6
ISBN 10: 1-57990-995-7

For information about custom editions, special sales, premium
and corporate purchases, please contact Sterling Special Sales
Department at 800-805-5489 or specialsales@sterlingpub.com.

Contents

Plain paper *(photo A)* can be transformed into one-of-a-kind crafting material with Krylon Paper Finishes. **Webbing Spray** *(photo B)* can create a soft texture or even a snow-like appearance. **Make it Stone!®** Metallic Textured Paint adds an opulent feel to projects *(photo C)*. Lapis Lazuli **Make it Stone!®** Textured Paint *(photo D)* was used on the Birthday Boy Box *(page 50)*.

A

B

C

D

Introduction

Paper Crafting Comes of Age

In 105 A.D., a mixture of mulberry, bark, hemp, and rags became the first documented sheet of paper. In the 2,000 years since, paper has been a cherished commodity in our lives, and today, this widely available medium allows us to freely express our creative spirit.

Today, tender memories are carefully saved and preserved on the pages of scrapbooks; cherished greetings are sent on beautifully designed greeting cards; and paper art decorates the nooks and crannies of our lives and our homes.

Paper's versatility and accessibility make it the most common art material today, but something wondrous and magical occurs every time an ordinary 8½" x 11" sheet of paper is transformed into something

extraordinary. Part of the magic of paper is that it's readily available and anyone, from experienced artists to beginning crafters, can express their creative vision with this simple medium.

Making beautiful art accessible is an important mission for Krylon, a company with a long tradition of working closely with major museums and other institutions for the preservation of fine art. In 1947, Krylon introduced its first product—a brush-on acrylic coating used by artists to preserve fine art.

Today, as the world's leading manufacturer of aerosol paint and coatings, Krylon's state-of-the-art, easy-to-use products are utilized by everyone, from dedicated artists to home hobbyists. Toward this end, Krylon introduced *Paper*

Finishes, a collection of paints, adhesives, and specialty coatings that are acid-free and archival-safe for scrapbooking and other paper crafts. It was with these products that all of the projects in this book were created.

Paper Finishes help you create with ease and style. The three-ounce cans are the perfect size for paper crafts, and the wide assortment of colors and finishes enhance your creative vision. From the vivid hues of *Stained Glass Sheer Color* to the soft, pearly sheen of *Make It Pearl!*, *Paper Finishes* will help transform your paper crafts from mundane to masterpiece. With just a spritz and a spray, hard-working *Paper Finishes* let you master any creative challenge.

Chapter 1

MATERIALS & TECHNIQUES

Adhesives:

• *Easy-Tack™* Repositionable Adhesive has a smooth, flexible, and temporary hold—great for holding in place stencils or masks. Use it to arrange your design elements temporarily, or for moving photographs, text, and other items until you're satisfied with the layout.

• *Adhesive Spray* offers a smooth, non-staining, and permanent hold that won't wrinkle. Ideal for paper and holds vellum fast with no show-through.

Preservation:

• *Make It Acid-Free!®* neutralizes the acids that occur naturally in paper and slows the aging process so papers do not become brittle. Spray ticket stubs, wedding announcements, report cards, and other paper mementos with *Make It Acid-Free!®* before you display them in your scrapbook.

• *Preserve It!® Digital Photo & Paper Protectant* adds a clear coating that will help preserve photographs and journaling text. *Preserve It!* shields your photographs and other printed documents from moisture and UV fading, and more than doubles their life. It's also effective on commercially printed photographs. For crisp, readable text on vellum and transparencies, spray surface of pages before and after printing with *Preserve It!® Digital Photo & Paper Protectant*. With *Preserve It!,®* there's no need to purchase special inkjet transparencies.

• *Workable Fixatif* is a clear coating that protects chalk, charcoal, crayon, pastel, pencil, and watercolor accents and drawings and keeps them from smudging. If you change your mind, you can erase through it, rework your artwork, and then spray again.

Texture:

• *Make It Suede!®* Textured Paint has a soft, brushed finish that mimics luxurious suede and adds a touch of realism and dimension to your work, whether you're creating teddy bears or rugged mountain ranges.

• *Webbing Spray* is a permanent, textured finish that adds wisps of color, recreating the look of elegant, veined marble or the fun of cobwebs.

• *Make It Stone!®* Textured Paints spray on a beautiful stone-like texture in realistic, variegated hues. Use the stone texture to recreate the essence of a grand, old cathedral or a sandy beach. Create an instant snowfall—from scattered flurries to blinding blizzards—with a quick spritz of White Onyx *Make It Stone!®*.

• *Make It Stone!®* Metallic Textured Paints combine a textured finish with regal, metallic shades.

Metallics:

• *Premium Metallics* in Copper, Gold, and Silver add high-gloss, metallic bling that looks like the real thing. Spray on paper, buttons, photo corners, and other items for an instant metallic finish.

• *Glitter Spray* adds a sprinkling of shimmer in metallic shades.

• *Leafing Pens* offer a rich, metallic finish in five colors—18KT. Gold, Silver, Copper, Red Shimmer, and Pale Gold. The versatile, chiseled tip draws both fine and thick lines; ideal for writing titles, edging pages, or coloring embellishments.

Sheer Color:

• *Antiquing Spray* offers instant vintage charm. The spray-and-go, no-wipe formula instantly ages papers and other surfaces.

• *Make It Iridescent!®* imparts a reflective, rainbow hue that adds a transparent, gossamer sheen.

• *Make It Pearl!®* adds a pearly yet transparent topcoat to your paper project.

• *Stained Glass Sheer Color* is available in bright, translucent colors. Spray on papers, photographs, and transparencies for a colorful, see-through finish.

• *Whitewash Spray* is an opaque, matte finish that will subtly lighten your papers. Spray on one coat or several to get the exact shade you need.

Vibrant Color:

• *Short Cuts® Aerosol Paints* are available in a colorful palette of 30 shades, from Muslin and Sand to Hot Pink and Tanzanite. The high-gloss colors are fast drying.

• *Short Cuts® Brush-On Paints* in 1-ounce jars are sized just right for paper crafts. The high-gloss brush-on paints are a perfect match for *Short Cuts Aerosol Paints* and *Short Cuts Paint Pens*.

• *Short Cuts® Paint Pens* add a colorful dash wherever it's needed, and can be used to color small embellishments too.

TECHNIQUES

Spray painting is like so many other crafting techniques—always follow the instructions and practice first.

To start, read the label on the can for application instructions, drying time, and how long you should shake the can.

Generally, shake the can for two full minutes once you hear the mixing ball begin to rattle, and repeat for 10 seconds after each minute of use. **Note:** *Make It Stone!*® requires just 10 seconds of shaking.

Follow the recommendations on the can for weather conditions and for best results, do not spray paint during times of high humidity. Paint in a well-ventilated area and protect your work surface from overspray with a drop cloth or newspaper. (To help contain any overspray, we offer advice for creating your own spray booth in "Helpful Hints.")

To start the proper paint flow and to make sure you have shaken the paint enough, spray on sheet of scrap paper first, and then practice your spray painting technique. Spray 10" to 12" (or as specified on the label) from the project, starting off your project, then spray across your project in a sweeping motion, maintaining a constant distance from the item being painted. Do not apply in one continuous spray; instead, release the spray button after each pass. Overlap each pass by about a third to keep paint finish even and consistent. Apply paint in thin coats to avoid runs or drips. Continue in this fashion until the entire project has one coat of paint.

Allow the fresh paint to dry completely for the recommended amount of time before adding a second coat.

Repeat if necessary.

HELPFUL HINTS

• Create your own "spray booth" to make clean up easy. Select a cardboard box large enough to fit your project. In a well-ventilated area, set the box on its side on top of a drop cloth (to catch any accidental over spray). Place your project inside and spray.

• Use double-sided tape to secure lightweight materials to your work surface so they don't move around when you paint them. For small, hard-to-hold objects, try wrapping masking tape (sticky side out) loosely around your hand several times, overlapping it slightly to create a large, sticky surface.

Adhere the item to be painted on the tape and voilá! Painting becomes easier.

Slide the tape off when you're done (item still attached) and secure to a table or other surface to finish drying. Your hands will remain paint-free, which is good for you and the project.

• If you hate to wear gloves when painting, protect your hands with a barrier cream or other hand lotion before starting your project. If you get paint on your hands, it will be easier to wash off.

• Save plastic grocery bags—they're great for masking off

18 KT. Gold metallic spray paint transformed the plain white card base of the Initial Card. Gold Webbing Spray was added to the black velveteen scrapbook paper.

areas of a project when used with painter's masking tape and won't leave ink on your project the way newspaper does.

UNIQUE IDEAS

• **Marble Mania:** Hand-marbled paper is gorgeous, but time consuming. Take a short cut with *Paper Finishes.* Half fill an old dish tub, foil pan, or other container with water. Mix and match your color and finishes and heavily spray the surface of the water with two or three shades of *Stained Glass Sheer Color, Metallics,* and/or *Short Cuts®* aerosol paint. Swirl the paint with a toothpick or straw and then, working quickly, place paper on the surface of the water and submerge completely, transferring the marbled design. Remove the paper and let dry.

The paper used on the Advent Box was created with the marbling technique.

- **Masking**: This is the latest paper crafting craze. To secure your mask or stencil, spray it first with *Easy-Tack™* repositionable adhesive. Once your mask is in place, spray on the color with *Paper Finishes*, let dry, and remove.

- **Rubbed the Right Way**: With *Preserve It!*, a transparency, and an ink-jet printer, create your own custom rub-on transfers using custom phrases or photographs you designed with photo-editing software. To begin, spray a transparency with *Preserve It!®*, let it dry, and then feed it through your inkjet printer, transferring the image onto the side of the transparency that's been coated with *Preserve It!®* Spray again with *Preserve It!®* and let dry. Then, using a stylus or bone folder, rub the image onto paper, wood, plastic, or a painted surface.

Masking was used to create pages in the Travel Journal. Simply lay a scrap piece of paper over the area you want to block off, and spray the page. Remove this scrap paper to reveal the plain area underneath.

To create the Mosaic Purse, Make it Stone!® Metallic Gold and 18KT. Gold metallic spray paints were used on plain scrapbook paper that was die cut and adhered to a papier-mâché box.

The soft, ethereal look of the Beauty and Love card was achieved by applying pearlescent spray paint over the card after it had been stamped and embellished.

SUPPLIES

Acetate: Available in sheets and rolls. Used with leafing pens, paint, and stamps.

Alcohol ink: Acid-free, fast-drying, permanent, and transparent, dye inks formulated to create a vibrant, polished stone look. Use on glossy paper, dominoes, and other slick surfaces.

Alcohol ink blending solution: Used to dilute and lighten alcohol ink. Also can be used to clean alcohol ink from hands, surfaces, and tools.

Bristle brushes: Paintbrushes with synthetic or natural bristles.

Cardstock: Medium-weight to heavyweight paper used in creating projects.

Craft glue: White glue used to adhere embellishments and papers to project surfaces.

Craft knife: Used to make precision cuts; has a razor-sharp edge attached to a narrow handle for easy control.

Craft mesh: Self-adhesive, repositionable decorative mesh used to create three-dimensional embellishments.

Deckle-edge scissors: Used to create a decorative edge as you cut. Also used as a guide for creating unique torn edges.

Decoupage medium: Thick, spreadable glue and sealer used to adhere and seal papers to project surfaces. Available in gloss, matte, and satin finishes.

Double-sided tape: Used to adhere papers and lightweight embellishments to projects. Use acid-free, permanent tape.

Drill and drill bits: Used to make holes for nails and screws.

Drywall tape: Tape with holes. Add to pages and paper projects for extra dimension. Can be inked, painted, or stained.

Felt-tip pens: Used to add journaling on pages and tags.

Foam dots: Used to adhere paper and embellishments to projects. Adds dimensional effect by lifting item off surface.

Gel medium: Used to create thick transparent glazes, add dimension to paint, enhance colors and textures, and extend paint drying time.

Glue dots: Flat, sticky adhesive dots used to adhere papers and non-porous embellishments (like plastic and metal) to projects.

Inkpads: Used alone or with stamps to decorate papers, projects, and tags.

Latex gloves: Used to protect hands from overspray.

Masking tape: Used to mask off areas of projects to protect from paint.

Newspaper and wax paper: Used to protect work surfaces. First secure newspaper to top of work surface then lay wax paper on top of wax paper. Use the wax paper as a "turn table" to turn projects as you apply spray paint and paper finishes.

Old box: Used to create spray booth to protect areas from overspray.

Paper punches: Used to cut holes in scrapbook pages and tags. Corner punches are used for rounding corners of papers and tags.

Paper towels: Used in creating projects and for clean-up.

Paper trimmers and scissors: Used for cutting paper and other materials.

Photographs: Use color, black-and-white, or sepia-tone copies of photographs when creating scrapbook pages and other projects.

Pounce or stencil brushes: Round, thick bristle or foam brushes used to apply paint directly onto stencils.

Rubber stamps: Used with inks and leafing pens to decorate papers.

Rulers: Used for accurate measurements and as a guide for tearing papers. Metal rulers work well for both purposes.

Sandpaper: Used for smoothing wood surfaces and distressing papers. Fine-grit sandpaper works best for projects in this book.

Scrapbook paper: Decorative, text-weight paper used in creating projects.

Soft cloths: Used to create paint effects and wipe dust from projects. Use lint-free cloth.

Stickers: Used to embellish papers and projects.

Stylus: Pointed instrument used to incise lines on soft surfaces.

Vellum: Translucent paper available in solids and prints.

Wet wipes: Used to apply paint and for clean-up of hands, tools, and work surfaces.

Let your photographs
be the star attraction
by creating custom
background papers
and photo mats.

Chapter 2

SCRAPBOOKING IDEAS

We scrapbook for many reasons—from preserving family history to celebrating friendships and events. We catalog our lives with photographs and mementos, select just the right materials to express our sentiments on each page, and then spend hours putting it all together. Brads, eyelets, embellishments, inks, paints, pretty papers—these are standard elements for scrapbook pages.

But how do you take scrapbooking to the next level? Bring unique, updated treatments to your layouts with spray paint and paper finishes.

In this chapter we add spray paint and other spray paper treatments to your treasure chest of ideas for creating scrapbook pages that uniquely capture your special memories. Recall a day at the beach with real sand texture, or a day on the slopes with "snow-capped" pages. Use stained glass color paint to create eye-popping slide mounts. Make "lace" paper with webbing texture. Paint edges of pages, mats, and embellishments with leafing pens. Use some of the hottest techniques in scrapbooking today including masking and dimensional effects.

Learn how to make specialty papers with textured finishes and paints; preserve digital photographs, newspaper clippings, and artwork with protective coatings; and how to use adhesive sprays to hold it all together.

French RIVIERA

CÔTE D'AZUR   CÔTE D'AZUR   CÔTE D'AZUR

SUN

SEA

LA RÉSERVE DE NICE

GRAND RESTAURANT SUR LA MER

Faux stone spray paint creates the texture on the slide mounts. Leafing pens are used to edge the photographs, photo mats, postcard, and slide mounts, and tie all of the elements together.

French Riviera

INSTRUCTIONS

1. Cut 4" x 12" strip of script scrapbook paper. Adhere to top of weathered natural cardstock using adhesive spray. (This is the background page.)

2. Ink edges of script scrapbook paper with sepia-tone ink. Paint edges of background page with gold leafing pen.

3. Using black inkpad, repeatedly stamp "Cote D'Azur" across 12" length of twill ribbon. Cut twill into two sections and attach to copper ribbon slide. Adhere stamped twill ribbon pieces at seam on background page using double-sided tape.

4. Spray book pages with acid-free spray. Tear and adhere torn book pages to chipboard base using gel medium.

5. Thin acrylic paint with water then wash chipboard with paint using sponge brush.

6. When chipboard is completely dry, cut into random square and rectangular shapes to fit letter stamps and slide mounts. Sand surface of each shape, then apply sepia-tone ink around edges. Let dry, then paint edges with copper leafing pen.

7. With acrylic paint, stamp title letters "Riviera" and words "Sun" and "Sea" onto chipboard pieces. With black ink, stamp word "French." Arrange, then adhere to background page using foam dots.

8. Spray slide mounts with faux stone texture. Let dry, then wash with acrylic paint to coordinate with patterned papers. Paint edges of slide mounts with copper leafing pen. Adhere to small photograph and words, "Sun" and "Sea," using craft glue. Arrange, then adhere to background page using foam dots.

9. Cut two 4¼" x 6¼" pieces of glossy white cardstock. Add several drops each of eggplant and lettuce alcohol ink onto felt-tip applicator. Pounce randomly onto glossy cardstock. Add more ink, few dabs from copper and gold leafing pens along with few drops of alcohol ink blending solution, and go over entire piece, blending neatly; let dry. (These are polished stone backgrounds).

10. Cut two 4¼" x 6¼" pieces of dark brown cardstock. Mount 4" x 6" postcards on dark brown cardstock using adhesive spray. **Note:** If using an authentic antique postcard, treat it first with acid-free spray.

11. Next, mount these onto polished stone backgrounds using adhesive spray. Edge polished stone backgrounds and postcards with copper leafing pen. Adhere both mounted postcards to bottom portion of page using adhesive spray.

12. Adhere slide mount word accents to bottom portion of page using foam dots.

13. Attach fiber trim to postcard using copper mini spiral clip.

Materials

- Acid-free spray
- Acrylic paint: teal blue
- Adhesive spray
- Alcohol ink: eggplant, lettuce
- Alcohol ink blending solution
- Book pages
- Cardstock: dark brown, glossy white, weathered natural, 12"x 12" (1 each)
- Chipboard
- Craft glue
- Double-sided tape
- Faux stone spray paint: rose quartz
- Felt-tip applicator
- Fiber trim
- Foam dots
- Gel medium
- Ink: sepia tone
- Inkpad: black
- Leafing pens: copper, gold
- Mini spiral clip: copper
- Photograph: small
- Postcards (2)
- Ribbon: twill, ½" wide
- Ribbon slide: copper
- Rubber stamps: alphabet letters
- Sandpaper
- Scissors
- Scrapbook paper: natural color with script, 12"x 12"
- Slide mounts: plastic
- Sponge brush: 1"

Kaitlyn &
Ashley loved
Playing in
the sand
on the beach!

Parajo Dunes,
California
June '01

Faux stone spray paint is used to create the "sand"
at the bottom of the page. Die-cut sand dollars add to
the beach theme.

Keeping Things in Place

Use bits of glue dots to keep fiber
trim in place. These little dots are
wonderful at holding just about any
type of embellishment firmly in place
—from ribbons to shells to metal
tags. Because they are sticky, use a
craft knife to cut and place the bits
of glue dots onto the page.

Surf's Up!

INSTRUCTIONS

1. Cut one strip of light tan cardstock approximately 3" x 10" and another strip approximately 3½" x 10". Tear along one long edge of each piece. **Note:** The straight edge will run along the bottom of the scrapbook page.

2. Spray both strips and 5" x 7" piece of natural cardstock with light coat of faux suede spray paint; let dry. Spray back of 3½"-wide strip of cardstock with repositionable adhesive and position on bottom of light blue cardstock as shown. Place stick-on letters on 3"-wide piece of cardstock to make title. Spray piece with faux stone spray paint; let dry, then carefully remove letters to reveal suede texture underneath.

3. Die-cut large tag from suede-painted rectangle, then spray with one coat of faux stone spray paint; set aside to dry. Die-cut smaller tag from light blue cardstock and shade edges using blue pastel artist pen. Adhere blue tag to stone tag background with double-sided tape. Tear scrap of faux stone-painted paper and adhere to bottom of blue tag with double-sided tape.

4. Create miniature sand dollar from circle and flower punches (hand cut little indent along sides to match large die shapes). Add journaling and tie fiber trim to tag as shown.

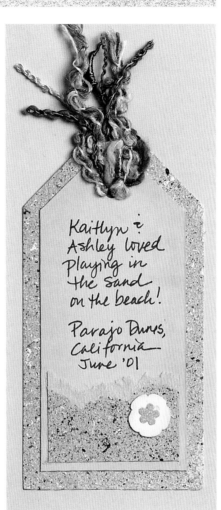

Materials

- Adhesive spray: repositionable
- Cardstock: light blue, light tan, medium blue, natural, 8"x 10" (1 each)
- Craft knife
- Die cuts: sand dollars, tags
- Die-cut machine
- Digital photo and paper protectant spray
- Double-sided tape
- Faux stone textured spray paint: travertine tan
- Faux suede textured spray paint: berber
- Fiber trim
- Glue dots
- Paper punches: circles, flowers
- Pastel artist pens: blue, sandy brown
- Photograph: 3½"x 5"
- Ruler
- Scissors
- Stick-on letters

5. Die-cut sand dollar shapes from faux suede-painted rectangle and natural cardstock. Carefully cut out centers from suede shapes with craft knife and adhere to center of natural cardstock shapes with glue dot. Shade with sandy brown pastel artist pen around edges.

6. Spray photograph with digital photo and paper protectant spray; let dry. Adhere to torn blue cardstock with adhesive spray. Attach to light blue cardstock as shown using double-sided tape.

7. Layer 3" strip of light tan cardstock at bottom of layout as shown using double-sided tape. Tuck in sand dollars; adhere with double-sided tape. Adhere tag to light blue cardstock using double-sided tape to complete project as shown.

Thank heaven for little girls. Echo the casual look of the photograph with denim-looking papers created using faux stone and faux suede spray paints.

My Girls

INSTRUCTIONS

1. Spray one sheet of medium blue cardstock with faux stone spray paint; let dry.

2. Spray one sheet of medium blue cardstock with faux suede spray paint; let dry.

3. Cut two 3" x 12" strips of faux stone-painted cardstock. Tear one long edge of each strip.

4. Cut two 3½" x 12" strips of faux suede cardstock. Tear one long edge of each strip.

5. Adhere strips of faux suede-painted cardstock, torn edges towards center of page, to piece of medium blue cardstock using adhesive spray. (This is the background page.)

6. Adhere strips of faux stone-painted cardstock to top of faux suede-painted cardstock using adhesive spray.

7. Die-cut tags from cardstock.

8. Die-cut title from foil. Spray back of letters with adhesive spray then adhere to oval tags. Add oval tags to background page using glue dots.

9. Cut one ¼" x 12" strip of faux suede cardstock. Adhere to middle of bottom faux stone-painted piece using adhesive spray. Adhere rectangle tags to strip using glue dots.

10. Add nailheads to top of oval tags and sides of square tags *(photo A)*.

11. Bend wire to form word "My." Cut two 1" pieces of wire and bend in half. Poke ends through word, then through paper. Adhere to back of page using double-sided tape.

12. Cut one 5½" x 7½" piece of medium blue cardstock. Cut one 5¼" x 7¼" piece of faux suede-painted cardstock then mount to medium blue cardstock using double-sided tape.

13. Spray photograph with digital photo and paper protectant spray; let dry. Mat photograph to 5¼" x 7¼" piece of faux suede-painted cardstock using double-sided tape. Adhere to background page using adhesive spray.

14. Cut two ¼" x 7" pieces of faux stone painted cardstock. Add strips of faux stone-painted cardstock to top and bottom of photograph using adhesive spray.

Materials

- Adhesive spray
- Adhesive tape
- Cardstock: medium blue (6)
- Die cuts: alphabet letters, oval tags, rectangle tags, square tags
- Die-cut machine
- Digital photo and paper protectant spray
- Double-sided tape
- Embossing foil
- Faux stone spray paint: metallic silver
- Faux suede spray paint: britannia blue
- Glue dots
- Nailheads: silver (7)
- Photograph: 5"x 7"
- Round-nose pliers
- Ruler
- Scissors
- Wire: silver, 24-gauge
- Wire cutter

Helpful Hints

Around the Edges

To achieve straight torn edges, use a metal ruler as your guide. If you prefer a design to your torn edge, use a metal ruler with a decorative edge. If you are tearing small pieces of paper, decorative-edge scissors can also be used as a guide.

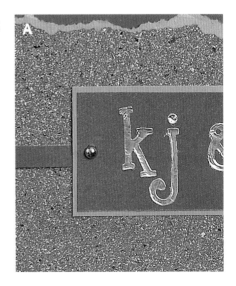

Simple Things in Life

Materials

- Adhesive spray
- Cardstock: dark gold, 12"x 12" (1); ivory, 12"x 12" (3)
- Chipboard letters
- Craft glue
- Digital photo and paper protectant spray
- Embellishments: leaves
- Faux suede spray paint: bordeaux, caramel
- Photographs: 3½"x 5", 3"x 4" (1 each)
- Rub-on letters
- Ruler
- Scissors
- Scrapbook paper: yellow patterned, 12" x 12"

Autumn leaves and fall colors reflect the colors and feel of the photograph. Chipboard letters tell the story of the day.

INSTRUCTIONS

1. Spray two pieces of ivory cardstock with bordeaux faux suede spray paint and one piece of ivory cardstock with caramel faux suede spray paint; let dry.

2. Trim dark gold cardstock to 11½" x 11½". Adhere to 12" x 12" piece of ivory cardstock using adhesive spray.

3. Trim caramel-painted cardstock to 11¼" x 11¼". Adhere to dark gold cardstock using adhesive spray.

4. Trim bordeaux-painted cardstock to 9¾" x 9¾". Adhere to caramel-painted cardstock using adhesive spray.

5. Trim scrapbook paper to 9½" x 9½". Adhere to bordeaux-painted cardstock using adhesive spray. (This is the background page.)

6. Spray both photographs with digital photo and paper protectant spray; let dry.

7. Cut one 3¼" x 4¼" piece of bordeaux-painted cardstock. Mount 3" x 4" picture to cardstock using adhesive spray.

8. Cut one 3¾" x 5¼" piece of bordeaux-painted cardstock. Mount 3½" x 5" photograph to cardstock using adhesive spray.

9. Adhere both mounted pictures to background page using adhesive spray.

10. Arrange chipboard letters and adhere to background page using craft glue; let dry.

11. Apply rub-on letters to background page.

12. Adhere leaf embellishments to background page with adhesive spray.

We Love Our Grandpa

Webbing texture and die cuts are used to create the papers in this layout. The simple design lets the photograph take center stage.

Materials

- Adhesive spray
- Cardstock: burgundy, dark green, 12"x 12" (1 each); dark blue, 12"x 12" (2)
- Computer and printer
- Die cuts: hearts
- Die-cut machine
- Digital photo and paper protectant spray: gloss finish
- Glue dots
- Nailheads: gold (4)
- Photograph: 5"x 7"
- Ruler
- Scissors
- Transparency film: 8½"x 11"
- Webbing texture spray: gold

INSTRUCTIONS

1. Spray one sheet of dark blue cardstock with webbing texture; let dry. (This is the background page.)

2. Spray one sheet of burgundy cardstock with webbing texture; let dry.

3. Cut one 6" x 12" piece of burgundy cardstock. Cut one 6½" x 12" piece of dark green cardstock; tear along both long edges. Using adhesive spray, mount burgundy cardstock onto dark green cardstock; adhere to background page using glue dots.

4. Die-cut hearts from dark green cardstock; adhere to burgundy cardstock using glue dots.

5. Spray transparency with digital photo and paper protectant; let dry. Using computer and printer, print text onto transparency film. Again, spray transparency with digital photo and paper protectant spray. Cut transparency film to 3¾" x 8½"; adhere to layout with nailheads.

6. Spray photograph with digital photo and paper protectant spray; let dry.

7. Cut 5¼" x 7¼" piece of dark blue cardstock. Mount photograph onto dark blue cardstock using adhesive spray; adhere to background page using glue dots.

blue jean babe

Eight years old
November 2004
photo: Chris Peters

Celebrate girlhood innocence with
this simple layout. The denim-looking
papers reflect the look of her jeans.

Blue Jean Babe

INSTRUCTIONS

1. Spray photograph with digital photo and paper protectant spray; let dry.

2. Place craft mesh on black cardstock and spray with whitewash spray then antiquing spray; let dry. When dry, remove craft mesh from page. (This is the background page.)

3. Spray dark blue and white cardstock with pearlescent paint; let dry.

4. Cut two 1½" strips and one 1" strip of dark blue cardstock.

5. Adhere 1½" strips down sides of background page as shown using double-sided tape.

6. Adhere 1" strip across top of background page as shown using double-sided tape.

7. Attach brads to background page as shown.

8. Cut one 5½" x 9" piece of white cardstock; this will be photo mat. Tear one short side to create uneven edge; torn edge will be the bottom of photo mat. Adhere to background page using adhesive spray.

9. Adhere photograph to white cardstock as shown using adhesive spray.

10. Die-cut title from dark blue cardstock. Adhere to photo mat as shown using adhesive spray.

11. Journal on background page as desired using leafing pen *(photo A)*.

12. Attach suspender clip and 4" length of ribbon to top of photograph *(photo B)*.

Materials

- Adhesive spray
- Antiquing spray
- Brads: star-shaped, gold (6)
- Cardstock: black, dark blue, white, 12" x 12" (1 each)
- Craft mesh: repositionable, self-adhesive, 12" x 12"
- Die-cut machine
- Die cuts: alphabet letters
- Digital photo and paper protectant spray
- Double-sided tape
- Leafing pen: silver
- Pearlescent spray paint
- Photograph: 5" x 7"
- Ribbon: light blue, ¼" wide, 4" length
- Ruler
- Scissors
- Suspender clip
- Whitewash spray

FISHIN
with daddy

Dave bought Taylor her very first fishing pole (Tweety Bird) and she couldn't wait to go fishing!

They bought some worms and headed off to the lake for their very first fishing adventure.   May 2001

Crumpled cardstock lends a natural feel to this page. The journaling tag tells the story of a very special day spent with Dad.

Fishin' With Daddy

INSTRUCTIONS

1. Crumple one sheet of white cardstock. Smooth out cardstock and spray with buckskin faux suede spray paint; let dry.

2. Spray two sheets of white cardstock with forest glen faux suede spray paint; let dry.

3. Using adhesive spray, attach crumpled cardstock to one sheet of forest glen-painted cardstock. (This is the background page.)

4. Cut one 3¼" x 7½" piece of forest glen-painted cardstock.

5. Cut one 2½" x 7¼" piece of white cardstock. Cut out letters f, i, s, h, i, n using alphabet letter die cuts. Spray cardstock piece with buckskin faux suede spray paint; let dry. When dry, attach this piece to 3¼" x 7½" forest glen-painted cardstock using foam dots. Using black felt-tip pen, write "with daddy" on forest glen-painted cardstock. Feed wire through "F" opening and hang fish stickers on each end.

6. Cut one 8¼" x 6½" piece of forest glen-painted cardstock.

7. Cut one 5¼" x 7⅛" piece of white cardstock. Spray with buckskin faux suede paint; let dry, then mount to 6¼" x 8½" forest glen-painted cardstock using adhesive spray. Spray photograph with digital photo and paper protectant spray; let dry.

8. Mount photograph on buckskin-painted cardstock using adhesive spray. Attach mounted photograph to background page using foam dots (*photo A*).

9. Cut one 5½" x 3½" piece of forest glen-painted cardstock. Tear one 3½" edge. Cut one 2¾" x 4½" piece of white cardstock. Journal as desired and mount on forest glen-painted cardstock using adhesive spray. Attach to background page using foam dots (*photo B*).

10. Cut one 12" x 5" piece of white cardstock. Crumple cardstock, smooth out, and then spray with buckskin faux suede paint; let dry, then tear along one long edge. Using nailheads, mount to top of page with straight edge at top.

11. Attach "Fishin with daddy" title to piece of crumpled paper at top of background page using foam dots.

Materials

- Adhesive spray
- Cardstock: white, 12"x 12" (5)
- Die cuts: alphabet letters
- Die-cut machine
- Digital photo and paper protectant spray
- Faux suede spray paint: buckskin, forest glen
- Felt-tip pen: black
- Fish stickers (2)
- Foam dots
- Nailheads: gold (2)
- Needle-nose pliers
- Photograph: 5"x 7"
- Ruler
- Scissors
- Wire: silver, 24 gauge, 5" length

Our Young Lady

Papers and flowers were distressed with sandpaper to enhance the vintage feel of this page. A recent photograph was printed in black and white and embellished with charms and tulle.

Materials

- Adhesive spray
- Antiquing spray
- Cardstock: 12" x 12", cream (2); lavender (1)
- Iron
- Leafing pen: gold
- Nailheads: heart-shaped, large (1), small (4)
- Paper towels
- Photograph: 4" x 6"
- Ruler
- Sandpaper
- Scissors
- Stickers: embossed flowers, letters
- Tulle: cream, 2" x 12"
- Whitewash spray

INSTRUCTIONS

1. Wet and crumple one piece of lavender and one piece of cream cardstock; lay flat to dry. Once dry, spray both pieces of cardstock with antiquing spray; let dry. When dry, distress both pieces with sandpaper.

2. Trim lavender cardstock to 11¾" x 11¾". Place lavender cardstock between two paper towels and iron to flatten.

3. Cut one 5" x 7" piece of distressed cream cardstock. Adhere photograph using adhesive spray. Center and adhere this piece to lavender cardstock using adhesive spray.

4. Spray embossed flower stickers with whitewash spray; let dry. When dry, distress with sandpaper. Adhere to lavender cardstock as desired.

5. Attach letter stickers for title as desired.

6. Attach bottom of lavender cardstock to 12" x 12" cream cardstock as shown using small nailheads. Center tulle at top of photograph as shown and attach to photograph using large nailhead. Place edges of tulle at top corners of page as shown; attach tulle and top corners of lavender cardstock to 12" x 12" piece of cream cardstock as shown using small nailheads.

7. Paint edges of 12" x 12" cream cardstock with leafing pen.

These Hands of Mine

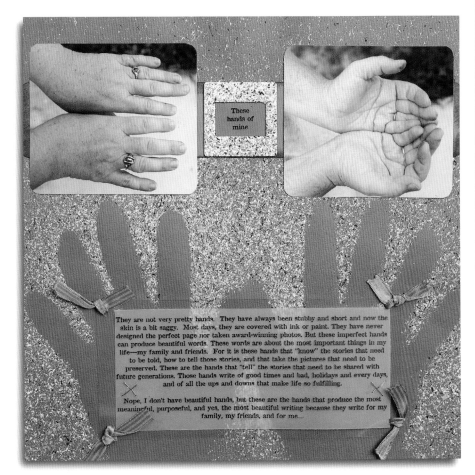

A writer's hands are celebrated on this page. Journaling was printed on vellum and simply stapled to the layout.

Materials

- Adhesive spray
- Cardstock: deep mauve, 12" x 12" (2)
- Computer and printer
- Craft paint: acid free brush-on, leaf green
- Digital photo and paper protectant spray
- Double-sided tape
- Faux stone spray paint: charcoal sand
- Latex gloves (1 pair)
- Paper punch: round
- Photographs: 4"x 4½" (2)
- Ribbon: ½" wide striped
- Ruler
- Scissors
- Slide mount: cardboard
- Sponge brush: 1"
- Stapler
- Staples: color of your choice
- Transparency film: 8½"x 11"
- Vellum: white, 8½"x 11"

INSTRUCTIONS

1. Wearing latex gloves, arrange hands on page and have friend spray page with faux stone spray paint. Lift hands off page and remove gloves; let page dry. (This is the background page.)

2. Spray slide mount with faux stone spray paint; let dry.

3. Spray photographs with digital photo and paper protectant spray; let dry.

4. Cut 2" x 12" strip of deep mauve cardstock. Round corners of strip with scissors. Using sponge brush, paint strip with craft paint; let dry. Attach to top of background page using adhesive spray.

5. Using computer and printer, print text for title (to go into slide mount) and story on transparency film. Trim title to 1" x 1½". Trim story text to fit over hands.

6. Adhere title and slide mount to center of strip using double-sided tape. Adhere photographs to strip using double-sided tape.

7. Punch hole in each corner of story transparency. Tie 3" piece of ribbon through each hole in transparency.

8. Cut piece of vellum ½" smaller than story transparency. Center vellum under transparency then staple both pieces to background page.

Mrs. Newton Rob Bommer
February 14, 2004

Prevent photographs from fading with digital photo and paper protectant spray. This page would make a lovely gift for a new bride.

Here Comes the Bride

INSTRUCTIONS

1. Cut five 1¼" squares, one 4¼" x 6¼" piece, and one 5¼" x 7¼" piece of black cardstock.

2. Spray white cardstock with thin layer of faux stone spray paint; let dry 15 minutes. Spray over texture with faux suede spray paint; let dry 15 minutes. Spray with digital photo and paper protectant spray; let dry 5 minutes. (This is the background page.)

3. Cut 2½"-wide ribbon to 14" length. Adhere ribbon down left side of page with adhesive spray.

4. Apply brush-on paint to wood flower, metal frame, and circle letter sticker. Use soft cloth to remove paint to achieve desired look; let dry.

5. Adhere 2" x 2" photograph to 2½" ribbon as shown using double-sided tape. Adhere metal frame on top of photograph.

6. Adhere one 1¼" square of black cardstock to 2½"-wide ribbon as shown using double-sided tape. Adhere metal frame on top of square as shown. Add letter sticker to center of frame.

7. Mount 4" x 6" picture to 4¼" x 6¼" piece of black cardstock. Adhere to background page with adhesive spray.

8. Mount 5" x 7" photograph to 5¼" x 7¼" piece of black cardstock as shown with adhesive spray. Tie 14" length of ½" wide ribbon around mounted photograph. Hold ribbon in place with metal square. Spray back of mounted image with adhesive spray and adhere to background page.

9. Using computer and printer, print text on transparency film. Cut transparency film to 4" x 6", spray back with adhesive spray, and lay on top of 4" x 6" photograph.

10. Cut 7" length of 1" wide ribbon. Spray back of ribbon with adhesive spray, arrange as desired, and adhere to textured cardstock. Attach wood flower to ribbon using glue dots. Add metal letter to top of flower.

11. Mount remaining small metal squares to 1¼" square black cardstock. Arrange and adhere to background page with glue dots.

Materials

- Adhesive spray
- Cardstock: black, white, 12"x 12" (1 each)
- Computer and printer
- Craft paint: acid-free brush-on, sun yellow
- Digital photo and paper protectant spray
- Double-sided tape
- Faux stone spray paint: sandy beach
- Faux suede spray paint: bordeaux
- Glue dots
- Letter sticker: circle
- Metal frames: adhesive-backed (2)
- Metal letter: adhesive-backed
- Metal squares: adhesive-backed (5)
- Photographs: 2"x 2" (1); 4"x 6" (1); 5"x 7" (1)
- Ribbon: ivory wired, ½", 1", 2½" wide
- Ruler
- Scissors
- Soft cloth
- Transparency film: 8½"x 11"
- Wood flower

A copper leafing pen was used to paint the edges of the photo mats, metal tags, letter stickers, and page corners, bringing all of these elements into one cohesive look.

Husband and Wife

Husband and Wife

INSTRUCTIONS

1. Spray both pieces of white cardstock and corrugated cardstock with forest glen faux suede spray paint; let dry. (Use one piece of forest glen-painted cardstock as the background page.)

2. Cut 4½" x 11¾" piece of plaid scrapbook paper; adhere to top of background page using adhesive spray.

3. Cut 8" x 11¾" piece of floral scrapbook paper; adhere to bottom of background page using adhesive spray.

4. Spray one piece of white cardstock with berber faux suede spray paint; let dry, then cut ¾" x 11¾" strip. Adhere strip on top of seam of two pieces of scrapbook paper using adhesive spray.

5. Spray photographs with digital photo and paper protectant spray; let dry, then adhere to background page using adhesive spray.

6. Cut 6" x 8" piece of corrugated cardstock. Using craft knife, cut 4" x 5¾" opening in center of piece.

7. Cut 5½" x 7½" piece of berber-painted cardstock. Using craft knife, cut 4" x 5¾" opening in center. Paint inner and outer edges with leafing pen. Cut 4¾" x 6½" piece of corrugated cardstock. Using craft knife, cut 4" x 5¾" opening in center. Paint inner and outer edges with leafing pen. (These pieces will serve as the frame for the large picture.)

8. Assemble picture frame pieces as shown. Join pieces together with adhesive spray, then adhere to background page.

9. Cut 3" x 7½" piece of corrugated cardstock. Tear one long side, right to left, and then down to bottom left edge. Adhere torn piece to bottom right corner of background page using adhesive spray.

10. Paint edges of metal corners, letters, and tags with leafing pen; let dry, then adhere to page.

11. Cut piece of floral scrapbook paper to fit inside medium tag. Adhere to tag using adhesive spray.

12. Using stamps and inkpad, add wording to inside of small tag. Add brad to inside of small tag.

13. Cut ribbon in half, then tie knot in center of each piece. Spray back of ribbon with adhesive spray, then place on page as desired (*photo A*).

Materials

- Adhesive spray
- Brad: small copper
- Cardstock: white, 12" x 12" (2)
- Corrugated cardstock: natural, 12" x 12" (2)
- Craft knife
- Digital photo and paper protectant spray
- Faux suede spray paint: berber, forest glen
- Inkpad: black
- Leafing pen: copper
- Metal corners: self-adhesive (3)
- Metal letters: self-adhesive
- Metal-trimmed tags: self-adhesive oval; small, medium (1 each)
- Photographs: 2" x 2" (2); 4" x 6" (1)
- Ribbon: wired leopard print, 2" wide
- Rubber stamps: small letters
- Ruler
- Scissors
- Scrapbook paper: floral, green plaid, 12" x 12" (1 each)

33

life

well lived

Mamie...the epitome of style, class, and boundless, warm, grandmotherly love.

A vintage sepia-tone photograph is perfectly complemented by the colors of the suede papers used behind it. Journaling was printed on transparency film and trimmed to fit the right side of the page.

Mamie

INSTRUCTIONS

1. Spray sheet of script scrapbook paper with water, crumple paper, and then iron flat. Spray paper with antiquing spray; let dry. Mount paper to black cardstock using adhesive spray. (This is the background page.)

2. Spray all sheets of velveteen paper with three colors of webbing texture; let dry.

3. Using leafing pen, paint metal corners, wording on stickpin, and buckle; let dry.

4. Cut 8½" x 10½" piece of ivory velveteen paper. Cut 8¾" x 10¾" piece of black cardstock. Mount ivory piece to black cardstock using adhesive spray. Adhere to background page with adhesive spray.

5. Cut 6½" x 8½" piece of rust velveteen paper. Cut 6¾" x 8¾" piece of black cardstock. Mount rust piece of paper to black cardstock using adhesive spray. Adhere to ivory paper using foam dots.

6. Spray photograph with digital photo and paper protectant spray; let dry. Adhere photograph to rust paper using foam dots.

7. Spray transparency film with digital photo and paper protectant spray. Using computer and printer, print text on transparency film. Again, spray transparency film with digital photo and paper protectant spray. Using embossing pen,

trace over letters. Apply embossing powder and set with heat gun. Trim film to 1½" wide. Adhere to background page using double-sided tape.

8. Cut two 1¼" x 10¾" strips of brown velveteen paper. Cut one strip with rounded end. Pull buckle through rounded end. Overlap pieces, making sure they reach to edges of page. Adhere to background page using double-sided tape *(photo A)*.

9. Adhere corners to ivory velveteen paper. Attach stickpin through fabric tag and rust velveteen paper *(photo B)*.

Materials

- Acrylic buckle: small
- Adhesive spray
- Antiquing spray
- Cardstock: black, 12"x 12" (4)
- Computer and printer
- Digital photo and paper protectant spray
- Double-sided tape
- Embossing pen: black
- Embossing powder: black
- Fabric tag
- Foam dots
- Heat gun
- Iron
- Leafing pen: 18KT. gold
- Metal corners: self-adhesive (4)
- Photograph: 5"x 7"
- Ruler
- Scissors
- Scrapbook paper: script; velveteen finish brown, ivory, and rust, 12"x 12" (1 each)
- Stickpin with wording
- Transparency film: 8½"x 11"
- Webbing texture spray: black, gold, white

Materials

- Adhesive spray
- Antiquing spray
- Brads (4)
- Cardstock: black, 12"x 12" (2); metallic copper, 8½"x 11" (6)
- Die cuts: leaves
- Die-cut machine
- Digital photo and paper protectant spray
- Double-sided tape
- Felt-tip pen: black fine-point
- Metallic spray paint: copper brilliance
- Photograph: 5"x 5"
- Ruler
- Scissors
- Whitewash spray

Metallic spray paint makes the elements on this page really pop. Remember the details of a girl's day out by journaling on the photo mat with a felt-tip pen.

Shades of Fall

INSTRUCTIONS

1. Spray one sheet of black cardstock with metallic spray paint; let dry.

2. Trim one sheet of black cardstock to 11¼" x 11¼" and mount to sheet of metallic copper cardstock using adhesive spray. (This is the background page.)

3. Spray two sheets of metallic copper cardstock with several light coats of antiquing spray. Spray another two sheets of metallic copper cardstock with several light coats of whitewash.

4. Die-cut several batches of leaves from one of each antiqued copper cardstock, metallic copper cardstock, and whitewashed metallic copper cardstock. Adhere leaves to background page using adhesive spray.

5. Cut four ¼" x 7¾" strips of black cardstock. Spray with metallic spray paint; let dry, then arrange into square on background page as shown. Adhere using double-sided tape. Attach brads at four corners of square. Add journaling to strips with felt-tip pen.

6. Cut 6½" x 6½" piece of metallic copper cardstock; adhere to

center of background page using adhesive spray.

7. Cut 6" x 6" piece of antiqued metallic copper cardstock; adhere to metallic copper cardstock using adhesive spray.

8. Cut 5½" x 5½" piece of black cardstock; adhere to antiqued metallic copper cardstock using adhesive spray.

9. Spray photograph with digital photo and paper protectant spray; let dry. Mount photograph to black cardstock using adhesive spray.

Pumpkin Time

The title on this page was created using stained glass sheer color spray paint. Notice how all of the elements reflect the colors in the photograph.

Materials

- Adhesive spray
- Cardstock: light yellow, 8½"x 11"
- Craft paint: brush-on acid-free sun yellow
- Die cuts: alphabet letters
- Die-cut machine
- Digital photo and paper protectant spray
- Glossy paper: white, 12"x 12"
- Paint pen: brown
- Paper punches: crescent, large circle, leaf stem, small circle
- Patterned paper: plaid, "trick or treat" (1 each)
- Photograph: 5"x 7"
- Ruler
- Scissors
- Sponge brush: 1"
- Stained glass sheer color spray paint: green, orange
- Transparency film: 8½"x 11"

INSTRUCTIONS

1. Spray transparency film with orange stained glass sheer color spray paint; let dry.

2. Spray white glossy paper with green stained glass sheer color spray paint; let dry.

3. Cut two 2" x 8" strips of plaid paper. Adhere to top and bottom of light yellow cardstock using adhesive spray.

4. Cut 6" x 8 " piece of "trick or treat" patterned paper and adhere to center of yellow cardstock with adhesive spray. (This is the background page.)

5. Spray photograph with digital photo and paper protectant spray; let dry. Adhere photograph to right-hand side of background page as shown using adhesive spray.

6. Sponge or brush on yellow craft paint in three areas on "trick or treat" patterned paper; let dry. After paint has dried, add journaling with brown paint pen.

7. Die-cut "Pumpkin Time" from orange-painted transparency film. Spray back of letters with adhesive spray then adhere to plaid borders.

8. Punch large and small circles and crescent shapes from orange-painted transparency film and overlap pieces to create pumpkin designs. Spray back of circles with adhesive spray then adhere to plaid borders.

9. Punch "stems" from green-painted glossy paper (trim away leaf part of stem leaf punch and use only stem portion). Spray back of stems with adhesive spray then adhere to top of pumpkins.

TOYS

Gold textured spray paints were used to create all of the papers seen here. Gold inks were used to paint the stencils and embellishments, tying all of the elements together.

Toys!

INSTRUCTIONS

1. Spray charms with metallic spray paint.

2. Paint outside edge of dominoes with leafing pen.

3. Cut four 1¾" squares of black cardstock. Stencil title letters on black cardstock then spray with metallic spray paint. Paint edges of each square with leafing pen *(photo A)*.

4. Place metal screen on ivory cardstock and spray with metallic spray paint. Remove screen; let dry. (This is the background page.)

5. Spray webbing spray on black cardstock; let dry. Tear 2½" x 12" strip. Attach strip to center of background page using adhesive spray.

6. Spray faux stone spray paint on white cardstock; let dry, then tear corners for upper right and lower left corners of layout. Paint sides and torn edges of corners with leafing pen.

7. Spray glitter spray on black cardstock and miniature playing cards; let dry, then paint edges of playing cards with leafing pen.

8. Spray photograph with digital photo and paper protectant spray; let dry, then paint edges with leafing pen.

9. Using deckle-edge scissors, cut 7" x 7½" mat for photograph from glittered black cardstock. Mount photograph onto mat using adhesive spray.

10. Place bingo card on background page as desired; adhere using adhesive spray *(photo B)*.

11. Adhere mounted photograph to background page using adhesive spray *(photo C)*.

12. Adhere corners at upper right and lower left using adhesive spray.

13. Fan out playing cards then attach brad. Adhere playing cards to lower left gold corner using craft glue.

14. Adhere charms, dominoes, and title letters to background page using craft glue.

Materials

- Adhesive spray
- Bingo card
- Brad
- Cardstock: black, ivory, white, 12"x 12" (1 each)
- Charms: crayon, dominoes
- Craft glue
- Deckle-edge scissors
- Digital photo and paper protectant spray
- Dominoes: small (2)
- Faux stone spray paint: metallic gold
- Glitter spray: glistening gold
- Leafing pen: 18KT. gold
- Metal screen: 12"x 12"
- Metallic spray paint: 18KT. gold
- Miniature playing cards (3)
- Photograph: 6"x 6½"
- Ruler
- Scissors
- Stencils: alphabet letters
- Webbing texture spray: gold chiffon

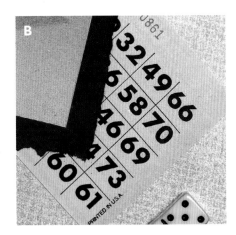

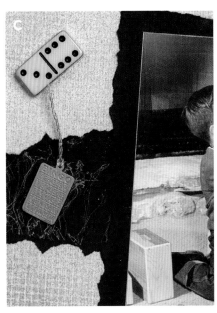

Mike & Santa
Dec. 1954

Stained glass sheer color spray paint was used to paint transparency film a brilliant red. The film was then used in slide mounts and as the photo mat. The black-and-white photograph was printed onto a clear transparency and mounted on gold cardstock for a stunning result.

Mike & Santa

INSTRUCTIONS

1. Spray 12" x 12" piece of white cardstock and all slide mounts with metallic spray paint (cardstock will be used for photo mat); let dry.

2. Spray 12" x 12" piece of white cardstock with glitter spray. (This is the background page.)

3. Using computer and printer, print journaling text on clear transparency film. Spray film with glitter spray and trim to 2¾" x 5½". Mask off words and spray edges of film with metallic spray paint; let dry.

4. Spray 12" x 12" piece of white cardstock with faux stone spray paint; let dry. Tear two ¾" x 12" strips for side borders.

5. Spray two sheets of transparency film with stained glass sheer color; let dry.

6. Cut ¾" x 6½" strip of red-painted transparency to fit behind title.

7. Cut three squares of red-painted transparency film to fit in slide mounts. Stamp with holiday-themed stamps and spray with digital photo and paper protectant spray; let dry, then insert into slide mounts (photo A).

8. Using piercing tool, make two holes at bottom of top slide; make two holes at top and two holes at bottom of middle slide; and two holes at top of bottom slide. Connect slides to jump rings with needle-nose pliers.

9. Spray remaining transparency film with digital photo and paper protectant spray; let dry. Print photograph on transparency film. Spray again with digital photo and paper protectant spray; let dry, then trim to edges of photograph.

10. Cut 5½" x 7½" piece of gold-painted cardstock. Mount photograph using adhesive spray.

11. Cut 6½" x 8¼" piece of red-painted transparency film. Attach to background page using adhesive spray. Attach mounted photograph to red-painted transparency film using adhesive spray.

12. Using adhesive spray, attach slide mounts, strips of metallic paper, strip of red-painted transparency film, and title to page.

13. Attach nailheads to sides of title and corners of photograph (photo B). Add rhinestones to each slide mount.

Helpful Hints

Transparent Colors

This layout could be adapted to most any holiday or seasonal celebration. Paint transparency film green, blue, and yellow for spring, blue and red for summer, or orange and yellow for fall. Of course red is the color of love and perfect for a Valentine's Day-themed page.

Materials

- Adhesive spray
- Cardstock: white, 12"x 12" (3)
- Computer and printer
- Digital photo and paper protectant spray
- Faux stone spray paint: metallic gold
- Glitter spray: glistening gold
- Inkpad: black
- Jump rings: gold (12)
- Masking tape
- Metallic spray paint: 18KT. gold
- Nailheads: gold (6)
- Needle-nose pliers
- Photograph: 5"x 7"
- Piercing tool
- Rhinestones: self-adhesive red (3)
- Rubber stamps: holiday-themed (3)
- Ruler
- Scissors
- Slide mounts: large cardboard (3)
- Stained glass sheer color spray paint: red
- Transparency film: clear, 8½"x 11" (4)

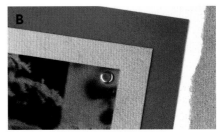

tis the season for

magical memories

taylor & santa 2002

Display magical memories as part of your holiday décor. Leafing pens and texture spray paints were used to create this stunning photo mat. Die-cut stars were wrapped with beaded gold wire.

'Tis the Season

INSTRUCTIONS

To create background page:

1. Crumble and slightly tear 12" x 12" cream cardstock. Flatten cardstock and lightly spray with berber faux suede spray paint; let dry.

2. Adhere berber-painted cardstock to red cardstock using one nailhead in each corner. (This is the background page.)

3. Add sequins and rhinestones to background page with craft glue.

To create title:

1. Cut 3¼" x 5" piece of vellum. Tear each short side to create uneven edge.

2. Using computer and printer, print "Magical" onto 8" x 10" piece of cream cardstock. Cut out letters using craft knife. Spray letters with black faux suede spray paint; let dry. Spray letters with webbing texture; let dry. Apply adhesive spray on back of letters and adhere to vellum as shown.

3. Write "'Tis the season for memories" on vellum as shown using felt-tip pen.

4. Adhere title to background page with glue dots.

To create stars:

1. Die-cut three star shapes from black cardstock. Using stylus, draw line (score) from center of each star to each point. Gently fold points of each star on scored lines.

2. Spray stars with light coat of glitter spray.

3. Cut three 5" strips of wire. String beads onto each wire. Wrap stars with beaded wire, tucking ends behind each star.

4. Secure stars to background page using glue dots.

To create photo mats:

1. Cut 6" x 8" piece of cream cardstock. Color edges using copper, 18KT. gold, and silver leafing pens; let dry.

2. Cut 5½" x 7¼" piece of black cardstock. Spray with webbing texture; let dry.

3. Cut 4¾" x 6¾" piece of cream cardstock. Spray with berber faux suede spray paint; let dry.

4. Mount mats, smaller to larger, using adhesive spray.

5. Spray photograph with digital photo and paper protectant spray; let dry. Mount photograph to mats using adhesive spray.

6. Attach one nailhead to each corner of mats as shown. Adhere to background page using glue dots. Trim bottom edge as shown.

To create tag:

1. Die-cut two ivory tags, one slightly smaller than other. Spray small tag with berber faux suede spray paint; let dry. Adhere to larger tag using adhesive spray. Trim outside edge of larger tag with copper and gold leafing pens. Trim outside edge of smaller tag with silver leafing pen.

2. Tear strip of vellum to fit tag; adhere to tag using double-sided tape. Journal on vellum as desired. Set eyelet in tag.

3. Cut 9" length of wire and string through eyelet. String beads on wire. Turn ends of wire with round-nose pliers to prevent beads from falling off. Twist wire as desired. Adhere tag to background page using glue dots.

Materials

- Adhesive spray
- Beads: small red (35)
- Cardstock: black, cream, red, 12"x 12" (1 each); cream, 8"x 10"
- Computer and printer
- Craft glue
- Craft knife
- Craft wire: gold, 24-gauge, 2 ft.
- Die cuts: stars, tags
- Die-cut machine
- Digital photo and paper protectant spray
- Double-sided tape
- Eyelet: star-shaped
- Eyelet-setting tools
- Faux suede spray paint: berber, black
- Felt-tip pen: fine-point black
- Glitter spray: gold
- Glue dots
- Leafing pens: copper, 18KT. gold, silver
- Nailheads: gold (8)
- Photograph: 4"x 6"
- Rhinestones: red (3)
- Round-nose pliers
- Ruler
- Scissors
- Sequins: gold (4)
- Stylus
- Vellum: white, 8"x 10"
- Webbing texture spray: gold
- Wire cutter

Chapter 3

MINI BOOKS & ALTERED BOOKS

Miniature books and altered books have become increasingly popular in recent years. Mini books can be created from cardstock, paper bags, and even pre-made kits. Altered books start life as novels, children's board books, and composition books, just to name a few examples.

No matter what their beginnings, these little books provide the opportunity to document your most personal thoughts, ideas, and memories more extensively than you can with traditional scrapbook pages. Because you are the author, your own book can be anything you want it to be: big or small, simple or intricate, full of bright colors or subtle neutrals.

Embellishments can range from stickers and photographs to game pieces and other found objects. Throw spray paint and paper finishes into the mix and the possibilities are endless. You are no longer limited by the availability of a certain decorative paper or other store-bought elements. Use spray paints and paper finishes to create your own papers, pages, and embellishments.

In this chapter you will learn to make a golf-themed paper bag journal, transform a composition book into a travel journal, use a children's board book as the base for a book about the game of life, and create a birthday book with matching box that will be added to year after year.

The golf journal was made using ordinary brown paper lunch bags. Journal pages and sayings were printed in colored ink and added to pages and tags.

Golf Journal Lunch Bag Album

INSTRUCTIONS

To make lunch bag album:

1. Place lunch bags on top of each other, rotating openings (for instance, first bag opening to left bottom flap up, second bag opening to right bottom flap still up, and so forth until you have as many pages as you would like in your book).

2. Sew seam down middle of compiled stack of desired number of lunch bags.

To make pages:

1. Spray cover, all pages, and back of book with antiquing spray, making sure to vary coverage on pages; let dry.

2. Spray several pieces of natural cardstock with buckskin faux

suede spray paint; let dry. Repeat three times, allowing paint to dry between coats.

3. Spray several pieces of natural cardstock with forest glen faux suede paint; let dry. Repeat three times, allowing paint to dry between coats.

4. Spray locknut and light switch cover with gesso; let dry. Spray locknut and light switch cover with buckskin faux suede paint; let dry. **Note:** The gesso spray acts as a primer so the faux suede paint will adhere to the items.

5. Lay metal screen on top of locknut and light switch. Using pouncing sponge, apply inks through screen onto items. Remove screen; allow ink to dry.

6. Using computer, printer, and off-white cardstock create and print journal pages. Cut pages to fit album pages and stamp with golf image. Spray journal pages with antiquing spray; let dry.

7. Cut painted and patterned papers to fit album pages.

Spray papers with antiquing spray; let dry.

8. Adhere journal pages, painted papers, and patterned papers to album pages as desired using adhesive spray.

9. Using computer, printer, and off-white cardstock, create and print golf-themed definitions. Cut out individual definitions. Spray with antiquing spray; let dry. Adhere to pages as desired using double-sided tape.

10. Embellish pages as desired using stamps, stickers, golf memorabilia, light switch cover, and locknut. Adhere embellishments using glue dots, foam dots, or double-sided tape.

To create tags:

1. Using computer, printer, and off-white cardstock, create and print golf-themed verses. Cut verses into tag shapes. Spray tags with antiquing spray; let dry.

2. Using buckskin-painted and forest glen-painted cardstock,

Materials

- Adhesive spray
- Antiquing spray
- Book knob with screw: small
- Cardstock: natural, off-white, as many as needed to cover desired number of pages
- Computer and printer
- Double-sided tape
- Faux suede spray paint: buckskin, forest glen
- Fiber trim
- Foam dots
- Gesso spray
- Glue dots
- Ink: burgundy, gold, green, rust, sepia-tone
- Iron-on adhesive
- Light switch cover: single wide opening
- Locknut
- Lunch bags: brown, desired number
- Metal screen: 7"x 7"
- Paper punch: circle
- Pouncing sponge
- Ribbons: coordinating colors, assorted sizes
- Rubber stamps: alphabet letters, golf-themed, numbers
- Ruler
- Scissors
- Scrapbook paper: brown suede, golf-theme, harlequin, striped, as many of each as needed to cover desired number of pages
- Sewing machine
- Stapler
- Staples: desired colors
- Stickers: golf-themed

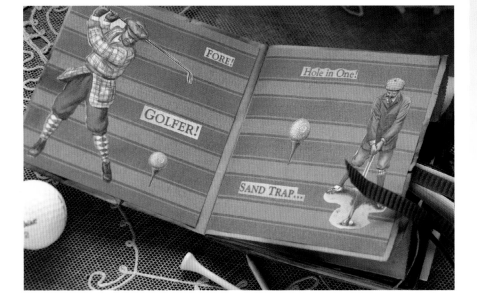

cut tag shapes slightly larger than verse tags. Adhere verse tags to these background tags using adhesive spray.

3. Using colored inks, color verse tags as desired; let dry.

4. Staple coordinating fiber and ribbon trim to top of tags as desired. Tuck tags into bag openings. Adhere a tag or two to album pages.

To create cover:

1. Cut two pieces of buckskin-painted cardstock, one to fit front cover and the other to fit back cover. Place screen on top of paper and spray paper with antiquing spray. Remove screen and let paper dry.

2. Cut piece of ribbon twice as long as needed for closure. Fold ribbon in half lengthwise. Adhere sides together using iron-on adhesive.

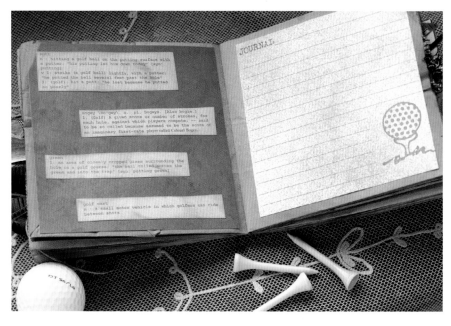

3. Cut 3" x 3" piece of buckskin-painted cardstock. Sew folded edge of ribbon to 3" x 3" piece of cardstock. Cut slice in ribbon ½" from top. (This is where the knob will pass through to close book.) Turn book over.

Adhere cardstock with ribbon to back cover using adhesive spray; let dry. Adhere cut piece of buckskin-painted cardstock to back cover using adhesive spray; let dry.

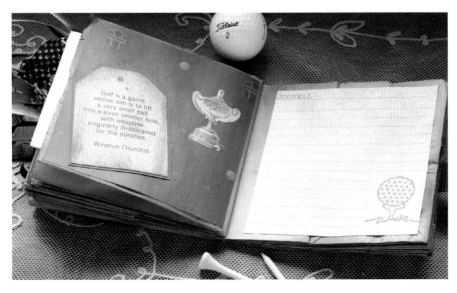

4. Turn book over. Adhere cut piece of buckskin-painted cardstock to front cover using adhesive spray. Punch hole half way down right side of cover, 1" in from edge. Push knob in hole and attach with screw.

5. Cut piece of brown suede scrapbook paper to wrap around spine of book. Cut piece of patterned paper of your choice slightly smaller than piece of brown suede paper. Adhere cut piece of brown suede paper to spine using adhesive spray. Adhere cut piece of patterned paper to brown suede paper using adhesive spray.

6. Cut three strips of forest glen-painted cardstock. Cut three strips of off-white cardstock slightly smaller than forest glen-painted cardstock. Spray off-white cardstock with antiquing spray; let dry.

7. Adhere forest glen-painted strips to front cover using adhesive spray. Adhere off-white strips to forest glen-painted strips using adhesive spray. Stamp words on strips as desired; let dry.

Helpful Hints

All Bound Up

Lunch bag albums can be bound in many different ways. You can punch holes down the seam, string ribbon through the holes, and knot the ends. Staples down the center seam are a fast, easy way to bind the book.

Materials

- Adhesive spray
- Bolts (2)
- Brads (4)
- Cardstock: tan, as many sheets as needed to complete your box
- Embellishments: bottle caps with stickers, miniature playing cards (ace and jack to say "21")
- Engraving tool
- Faux stone spray paint: lapis lazuli
- Glue dots
- Inkpad: brown
- Leafing pen: copper
- Leather belt buckle and tag
- Matte finish spray
- Metal letter charms: copper
- Ruler
- Sandpaper
- Scissors
- Screwdriver
- Screws (2)
- Stickers: clear numbers, boy-themed
- Wood box with hinges

The box top says "One 2 21." The belt buckle really works and serves as the clasp on the box.

Birthday Boy Box

INSTRUCTIONS

1. Spray box with three coats of faux stone paint; let dry thoroughly between coats.

2. Spray box with matte finish; let dry.

3. Cut piece of cardstock 3" wide x length of box plus 2". Spray back of strip with adhesive spray, and adhere to box approximately ⅓ of way from top. Wrap ends of strip around box and adhere to interior of box.

4. Attach metal letter charms to spell "celebrate" with brads. Paint brads with leafing pen.

5. Attach boy-themed sticker to front and add brads to top and corner as shown.

6. Using glue dots, attach bottle cap embellishments. Add stickers.

7. Ink surface of cards; let dry. Spray back of cards with adhesive spray and attach to box to represent "21."

8. Add stickers "One" and "2" to represent "1 to."

9. Engrave initials onto leather tag. Attach brads to corners of tag. Adhere tag to surface of box with glue dots.

10. Attach belt buckle and closure with screws and bolts.

11. Lightly sand edges and surface of box to achieve weathered look.

Birthday Boy Book

INSTRUCTIONS

1. Cut 6" x 6" piece of white cardstock.

2. Cut 6" x 7" piece of white cardstock. (How many you cut will depend on the child's age—one page for each year.) Using stylus, score and fold 1" over on all 6" x 7" pages so they measure 6" x 6".

3. Adhere small strip of one 6" x 7" piece of white cardstock to back of 6" x 6" white cardstock using adhesive spray. Repeat with all pages.

4. Cut and layer coordinating scrapbook papers as desired; adhere to cardstock with adhesive spray. **Note:** Each page will celebrate one birthday.

5. Stamp age of birthday year on page. Embellish with stickers. Repeat for each year.

6. Sand pages to distress; wipe with soft cloth.

7. Spray all pages with matte finish spray; let dry.

8. Spray all photographs with digital photo and paper protectant spray; let dry.

Use the same paper as the card to create a tag for every birthday. Journal about the day and then tuck the tag between the photograph and the card.

9. Cut mat for each photograph. Adhere photographs to mats using adhesive spray. Color edges of mats with ink, if desired.

10. Adhere matted photographs to appropriate pages using double-sided tape at top and bottom only. (This will create pocket for tags.)

Materials

- Adhesive spray
- Cardstock: coordinating colors; white
- Digital photo and paper protectant spray
- Double-sided tape
- Felt-tip pen: fine-tip black
- Fiber trim
- Inkpad: brown
- Leafing pen: copper
- Matte finish spray
- Paint pen: black
- Paper punch: circle
- Photographs: 1 for each year
- Rubber stamps: numbers
- Rub-ons: letters
- Ruler
- Sandpaper
- Scissors
- Scrapbook papers: coordinating polka-dot, solid, and striped
- Soft cloth
- Stickers: clear, numbers
- Stylus

11. Cut tag shapes from coordinating solid cardstock. Make sure tags fit into pocket behind photographs. Journal memories from each birthday on separate tags. Sand edges of each tag and wipe with soft cloth. Spray tags with matte finish spray; let dry.

12. Punch hole at top of each tag and tie fiber trim through holes. Slip tags behind pictures.

13. Using leafing and paint pens, add random copper and black lines on pages.

An old child's book with thick cardboard pages was used to create this altered book. A new book with thick pages would work just as well.

A

Life's-a-Game Book

INSTRUCTIONS

Note: Read through all of the instructions before beginning project.

To prepare book:

1. Lightly sand all surfaces of board book; wipe off dust with soft cloth.

2. Spray all surfaces of book with gesso; let dry. **Note:** Allowing gesso to run and accumulate on areas will add to the water-stained aged look.

3. Spray all surfaces of book with heavy coat of antiquing spray; let dry.

4. Ink edges of wood dominoes; let dry.

5. Using chalk inks, stamp harlequin image onto all surfaces and immediately wipe away. Ink will lift some of antiquing spray leaving tone-on-tone effect. **Note:** Use this technique throughout the book, randomly.

To make cover:

1. Cut out "game pieces" from scrapbook paper. Choose two to use on cover of book. Ink edges and adhere to book using adhesive spray. Using large foam stamps and craft paint, stamp "Life's a Game"; let dry. Shadow letters using felt-tip marker.

2. Arrange typewriter key letters, spelling "Play Hard" in crossword style, using same "A" in both words. Adhere to cover using glue dots (*photo A*).

Two pages were used to create the pocket page on the right-hand side. First, the top page was cut and then the pages were glued together on the sides and bottom.

To make pocket page:

Note: The set of two pages after the first page will be used to create a pocket page.

1. Using craft knife, carefully cut away half of first page, exposing second page. (Put cutting mat between pages to protect surface not to be cut.)

2. Adhere sides and bottom edges of these pages together with craft glue; let dry. **Note:** This creates a pocket to tuck in embellishments.

3. Using images cut from vintage games paper and wood dominoes, arrange simple collage and adhere to inside front cover (first page) using craft glue. Make sure to continue element of collage onto second page.

4. Using miniature playing cards, poker chips, vintage game images, fiber trim, and spiral clip, create collage. Adhere to page using craft glue. Embellish shipping tag by inking, stamping, and adhering playing card to it. Tuck shipping tag inside pocket. Using chalk inks, stamp words "Play by the Rules" on page. Finish this two-page spread by dipping eraser of pencil in off-white acrylic paint and stamping little circles around edges of both pages *(photo B)*.

5. The next page is a simple collage using more vintage game paper, a shipping tag, and sanded and inked puzzle pieces. Adhere collage pieces to page using craft glue; let dry.

Materials

- Adhesive spray
- Antiquing spray
- Cardboard: 8"x 8"
- Chalk ink: various colors
- Craft glue
- Craft knife
- Craft paint: brush-on, acid-free, off-white
- Cutting mat: self-healing, small
- Digital photo and paper protectant spray
- Double-sided tape
- Embellishments: bingo card, bingo numbers, game pieces, miniature playing cards, poker chips, puzzle pieces, spiral clip, typewriter key letters, wood dominoes
- Felt-tip marker: fine-point black
- Fiber trim
- Foam stamps: alphabet letters, large
- Gesso spray
- Glue dots
- Inkpad: black
- Leafing pen: copper
- Matte finish spray
- Pencil with round eraser
- Photograph
- Round board book
- Rubber stamp: harlequin
- Sandpaper
- Scissors
- Scrapbook paper: vintage games, 12"x 12"
- Shipping tags
- Soft cloth
- Strong-hold glue

To make frame page:

Note: The last set of two pages of the book will be used to create a frame page.

1. Using adhesive spray, cover inside of back cover (last page of book) with solid piece of scrapbook paper that has been distressed with sandpaper; let dry. Adhere vintage bingo card to inside back cover using adhesive spray; let dry.

2. Repeat directions for pocket page, except cut center from first page, leaving about 1" or so of frame. Adhere frame page to last page using craft glue; let dry.

3. On frame itself adhere more puzzle pieces, bingo numbers, and stamped word "bingo." For added interest, allow pieces to overlap to inside of frame *(photo C)*.

To finish book:

1. Spray all surfaces of book with matte finish; let dry.

2. Spray photograph with digital photo and paper protectant spray; let dry.

3. In frame page, adhere photograph using double-sided tape.

4. Paint all edges inside and out of book with leafing pen; let dry.

For added interest, layer puzzle pieces and other embellishments onto the inside page, not just the frame.

Travel Journal

INSTRUCTIONS

To make cover:

1. Cover front and back of composition book with gray scrapbook paper and maps. Papers and maps should overlap around edges and fold over to inside of book, completely sealing edges, and abut edges of book binding. Spray back of papers and maps with adhesive spray and adhere to book. Cover inside of covers by tearing edges of paper to fit; adhere using adhesive spray.

2. To create pocket on front of book, tear piece from map and adhere all but top edges with double-sided tape, allowing pocket to form. Ink and roll top edge of pocket.

3. Stamp pocket with travel images, then embellish with cheesecloth, metal stickers, tickets, and other items as desired.

4. Die-cut word "Journey" out of brown cardstock, spray back of letters with adhesive spray, and adhere to pocket.

5. Punch hole about 1" in from front edge of book using anywhere punch.

6. Punch 1" circle from brown cardstock, ¾" circle from patterned paper, and random shape from scrap of map. Layer these pieces and punch hole through center. Thread decorative brad through layers, adding clock hands between each layer. Insert brad into hole in cover; secure.

7. Embellish back of book with paper scraps and decorative brad.

To bind journal:

1. Spray tan cardstock with faux suede spray paint; let dry.

2. Gently crinkle cardstock, flatten, and spray with antiquing spray. Cut 4" x 11" rectangle from cardstock. Fold ¾" under on each narrow end. Spray back of rectangle with adhesive spray and adhere around binding so it is equal on each side.

3. Place cutting mat under cover. Using anywhere punch, punch holes every ½" through faux suede paper and cover of book. Do this on front cover and back cover.

4. Lace hemp twine through all layers and knot ends of twine.

Helpful Hints

Stable Beginnings

When altering a composition book, it is important to adhere two or three pages together to create more stability where you'll be adding embellishments or special effects. Use adhesive spray to adhere pages together.

Materials

- Adhesive spray
- Adhesive-backed notepad, small
- Antiquing spray
- Cardstock: brown, tan
- Chalk ink: earth tones
- Composition book: 8½" x 11"
- Cutting mat: self-healing
- Die cuts: alphabet letters
- Die-cut machine
- Embellishments: brads, clock hands, metal stickers, scraps of tea-stained cheese cloth, tickets
- Faux suede spray paint: caramel
- Hemp twine
- Inkpads: brown, green
- Maps
- Punches: anywhere; circles, ¾", 1"
- Rubber stamps: alphabet letters, number, travel-related
- Ruler
- Scissors
- Scrapbook paper: gray, patterned, travel theme
- Shipping tags: large, medium, small

This recreated composition book is now ready to hold memories from life's adventures.

photo A

To finish inside book:

1. Plan how to divide inside pages of book and label them with adhesive-backed notes. For example, you could divide your book into a section for each day of your vacation with a few pages in the front for topics like destination, agenda, etc.

2. On pages throughout book, stamp words depicting types of things you will document in your book, i.e. destination, agenda, etc.

3. Create an outlined effect on pages by tearing rectangle of scrap cardstock, smaller than page, and using it as a mask in center of page. Lightly spray page with antiquing spray, then remove mask to expose the journaling area.

To complete pocket pages:

1. Create side pockets by gluing three pairs of pages together, tearing them at different distances from binding to create layers. Add color with inks or paints. Staple, stitch, or adhere layers at top and bottom.

2. Embellish pages by stamping topics, travel quotes, and designs.

3. Ink shipping tags and tuck between layers for note taking. You could also tuck memorabilia inside these layers *(photo A)*. **Note:** Remember to adhere two or three pages together behind the layers for stability.

4. To create corner pockets, fold doubled page from top corner to about 2½" from opposite bottom corner. Embellish with patterned papers, paints, inks, etc. Stamp name of intended contents. This will create a great pocket to hold ticket stubs, brochures, and other treasures.

Paint edges of book and torn paper with chalk ink to give antique appearance.

To complete tabbed pages:

Note: Double up the first two pages in each section by adhering them together with adhesive spray. This will enable the pages to support the tabs and any photographs you may add.

1. Single page tabs: To create tabbed pages, fold about 1¼" under on side of page. Fold same amount of next page towards first. Adhere pages together with adhesive spray. Tuck small decorated tags between these layers in long row. **Note:** We used nine tags to spell out "Adventure" with one letter on each tag *(photo B)*.

2. Multi-page vacation day tabs: Divide remainder of book into amount of days you want to document. Ink edges of small shipping tags and stamp the word DAY on each one and then numbers representing day of trip i.e. 1-7 for a weeklong vacation *(photo C)*.

3. Using masking method described previously, mask off first page in each section and preceding page and lightly spray with antiquing spray.

Antiquing Effects

When using antiquing spray, you can achieve different effects by the way you control the nozzle. For an all-over smooth effect, spray lightly with nozzle completely pressed down. To achieve splattered, water-marked effect, barely hold the nozzle down—this causes it to spit and sputter the spray onto the page.

Creating handmade
cards and tags is fast
and easy. Giving one to
a cherished friend is
sure to make their day.

Chapter 4

CARDS & TAGS

In these times of mobile phones, fax machines, and email, there's nothing more special than a handwritten note or card. Imagine how wonderful it would feel to receive a handmade card or tag. Making cards and tags is also a wonderful way to be creative without a lot of time or a big financial commitment. And because they are simple to make, cards and tags are a great way to try paper crafting.

Cards and tags can easily be tailored to the receiver's personality. Pastel and soft colors, vintage-inspired themes, and embellishments speak to a more feminine mystique, while corrugated cardboard, heavy cardstock, and sports and fishing themes make great gifts for the men in your life.

In this chapter you will learn to use iridescent paint to add a soft shimmer, whitewash paint to soften colors, and antiquing spray for an aged appearance.

You also will learn how specialty techniques can be used to create truly unique projects: spray webbing texture and pearlescent paint on cardstock to create the unique papers used on the Initial Card; layer paints of all types and colors to achieve a glass-like look, like that seen on the Dream Card; and use gesso spray to ensure that paints will adhere to different paper types.

Beauty and Love Card

INSTRUCTIONS

To make card:

1. Lightly wipe front and back of card with craft paint using hand wipe; let dry.

2. Stamp desired image on front and back of card; let dry.

3. Tear piece of modern script paper to cover front of card. Adhere using adhesive spray; let dry.

4. Using gold leafing pen, paint torn edges of script paper and edges of card; let dry.

5. Spray front and back of card with pearlescent spray; let dry.

To make tag:

1. Paint entire shipping tag using craft paint and hand wipe; let dry.

2. Using craft knife, cut rectangle out of tag.

3. Cut piece of vellum slightly larger than rectangle and adhere to back of large tag using double-sided tape.

4. Spray photograph with digital photo and paper protectant spray; let dry. Attach photograph behind vellum using double-sided tape.

5. Cut piece of blue cardstock same size as shipping tag. Adhere to back of tag using double-sided tape.

(Opposite) Pearlescent paint gives this card and tag decidedly feminine flair. To further the soft look, a vintage photograph was mounted behind vellum.

6. Cut letters from modern script paper to spell "Beauty" and "Love."

7. Adhere small rectangle tag to shipping tag with eyelet. Adhere letters using craft glue.

8. Attach button to front of tag using craft glue; let dry.

9. Spray front and back of tag with pearlescent spray; let dry.

10. Paint small round tag with leafing pen; let dry, then adhere to top of shipping tag with double-sided tape.

11. Punch hole through small round tag. Tie fiber and ribbon trim through hole in tag.

12. Affix shipping tag onto front of card using brad *(photo A)*.

Materials

- Adhesive spray
- Blank card: off-white, 5"x 6"
- Brad
- Button
- Cardstock: blue, 8½"x 11"
- Craft glue
- Craft knife
- Craft paint: acid-free, bonnet blue
- Digital photo and paper protectant spray
- Double-sided tape
- Eyelet
- Eyelet setter
- Fiber and ribbon trim
- Hand wipe
- Inkpad: silver
- Leafing pen: gold
- Pearlescent spray paint
- Photograph: vintage
- Rubber stamp: your choice
- Scissors
- Scrapbook paper: modern, old-fashioned script
- Shipping tag: large
- Tags: small rectangle, small round (1 each)
- Vellum: off-white

A Great Gift

Cards with large tag embellishments are actually two gifts in one: the tags are removable and can be used as a bookmark. Just remember to write a note to the receiver so they know to remove the tag from the card.

Cigar Label Card

INSTRUCTIONS

1. Spray front and back of card with antiquing spray; let dry. Spray front and back of card with pearlescent paint; let dry.

2. Puddle quarter-size amount of both gold leafing pen and red shimmer leafing pen onto acetate. Wipe rubber stamps across acetate and then quickly stamp designs onto card front and back; let dry. Paint edges with gold leafing pen; let dry.

3. Cut 4¼" x 6⅛" piece of textured cardstock. Spray piece with buckskin faux suede spray paint; let dry. When dry, rub bordeaux ink on cardstock to achieve desired effect. Center this piece and adhere to front of card using adhesive spray.

4. Spray shipping tag with bordeaux faux suede spray paint; let dry.

5. Paint edges of tag using gold leafing pen; let dry.

6. Adhere patterned paper and cigar labels to shipping tag as desired using adhesive spray.

7. Adhere metal word tag to shipping tag.

8. Tie fiber trim to shipping tag.

9. Attach tag to card with brad.

The shipping tag on the Cigar Label Card was embellished with vintage cigar tags. You can also use cigar tag-themed collage paper.

Materials

- Acetate
- Adhesive spray
- Antiquing spray
- Blank card: off-white, 5"x 6"
- Brad: black, medium
- Cardstock: off-white, textured (1 each)
- Cigar labels: as many as desired
- Faux suede spray paint: bordeaux, buckskin
- Fiber trim
- Inkpad: bordeaux
- Leafing pens: 18KT. gold, red shimmer
- Metal word tag: self-adhesive, copper
- Pearlescent spray paint
- Rubber stamps: honeycomb, script
- Ruler
- Scissors
- Scrapbook paper: patterned
- Shipping tag: brown, large

Eye of the Soul Card

Materials

- Adhesive spray
- Blank card: white, 4"x 6"
- Cardstock: metallic silver, 8½"x 11"
- Embossing inkpad: black
- Embossing powder: black
- Glitter spray: silver
- Heat gun
- Metallic spray paint: 18KT. gold
- Paint styling spray
- Photo mat: black, pre-cut 3½"x 5",
- Rubber stamps: "Eye of the Soul" or other message, bird in flight
- Ruler
- Scissors
- Spray paint: flat white
- Stained glass sheer color spray paint: blue, green

INSTRUCTIONS

1. Spray cardstock with paint styling spray.
2. Immediately spray several coats of stained glass sheer color paints randomly over paint styling spray. While still wet, spray light layer of flat white spray paint, followed by metallic spray paint and glitter spray; let dry.
3. Cut painted cardstock to fit pre-cut black mat. Stamp card and emboss with embossing pen and powder.
4. Adhere stamped cardstock to mat using adhesive spray.
5. Adhere mat to blank card using adhesive spray.

Working quickly is the key to creating the unique finish on this card. A crystallizing technique was used to create the unusual pattern on the Eye of the Soul Card.

Initial Card

INSTRUCTIONS

To decorate outside of card:

1. Fold cardstock in half to form top-fold card base. Paint edges of card with leafing pen.

2. Cut one 5" x 8" and one 4" x 7" piece of black velveteen scrapbook paper. Spray both pieces with webbing texture; let dry. Adhere 5" x 8" piece to card using adhesive spray.

3. Cut 4½" x 7½" piece of patterned paper and spray with pearlescent spray paint; let dry.

Multiple layers and textures lend a rich look to the Initial Card.

Materials

- Adhesive spray
- Cardstock: off-white, 8½"x 11" (2)
- Computer and printer
- Decorative corners: metal, self-adhesive (4)
- Die cuts: letter
- Die-cut machine
- Fiber trim
- Foam dots
- Leafing pen: gold
- Metallic spray paint: 18KT. gold
- Paper punch: circle
- Pearlescent spray paint
- Scrapbook paper: aged (1), black velveteen (2), patterned (1), 8½"x 11"
- Shipping tag: large
- Webbing texture spray: gold

Adhere to card using adhesive spray. Adhere 4" x 7" piece of velveteen paper to patterned paper using adhesive spray. Paint metal corners with leafing pen and attach to card as shown.

4. Punch corners of shipping tag using paper punch. Cut piece of patterned paper slightly smaller than tag and adhere to tag using adhesive spray. Paint edges of tag using leafing pen. Spray tag with pearlescent spray; let dry.

5. Die-cut desired initial from cardstock. Paint initial with metallic spray paint; let dry. Adhere to tag using foam dots.

6. Tie fiber trim to top of tag. Adhere tag to card as shown, using foam dots.

To decorate inside of card:

1. Using computer and printer, print desired message onto aged scrapbook paper.

2. Cut 5¼" x 8¼" piece of off-white cardstock and paint edges with leafing pen.

3. Cut message to fit onto cardstock and adhere using adhesive spray.

4. Adhere to inside of card using adhesive spray *(photo A)*.

Elizabeth,

There is no limit to the goals you can attain,
The success you can achieve...
The possibilities are as endless as your dreams.

Congratulations
on your Graduation!

Iridescent Music Card

INSTRUCTIONS

1. Cut 6" x 12" piece of white cardstock and fold in half to create 6" x 6" top-fold card.

2. Cut 5½" square from black cardstock.

3. Cut 5" square from scrapbook paper. Adhere to 5½" square of black cardstock using adhesive spray. Adhere both to card using adhesive spray.

4. Cut 3" square from black cardstock.

5. Cut 2½" square from black patterned paper and spray with iridescent spray; let dry. Adhere to 3" square black cardstock using adhesive spray. Turn square on diagonal as shown and adhere to card using adhesive spray.

Materials

- Adhesive spray
- Cardstock: black (2), white (1)
- Glue dots
- Inkpad: black
- Iridescent spray paint
- Nailhead: music clef or note
- Rubber stamp: music definition
- Ruler
- Scissors
- Scrapbook paper: black patterned
- Slide mount: cardboard

6. Cut 2½" square from black cardstock. Spray with iridescent spray; let dry. When dry, adhere to center of card as shown using adhesive spray.

7. Stamp music definition onto slide mount and adhere to center of black square using glue dots.

8. Attach nailhead to center of card.

Only one patterned paper was used on this card—the color change is the result of iridescent spray paint.

Iridescent Effects

Iridescent spray can be used over paint or paper to completely transform a ho-hum project into one where the colors jump off the page. Apply one coat to allow original colors to show through or apply multiple coats for a more opaque appearance.

Stained glass sheer color paint was sprayed on glossy cardstock, resulting in the glass-like look on the Dream Card.

Materials

- Adhesive spray
- Beads: blues, purples (10-15)
- Cardstock: off-white, glossy dark purple, glossy white, 8½"x 11"
- Craft glue
- Craft knife
- Craft wire: 20 gauge, metallic copper
- Die cut: star embossing plate
- Die-cut machine
- Gel ink pen: gold
- Leafing pen: 18KT. gold
- Metallic leafing
- Needle-nose pliers
- Ruler
- Scissors
- Scrapbook paper: metallic copper, 8½"x 11"
- Stained glass sheer color spray paint: blue, green, purple
- Stylus

Dream Card

INSTRUCTIONS

Creating the card:

1. Cut 6½" x 10" piece of glossy dark purple cardstock and 6½" x 10" piece of scrapbook paper. Spray back of papers with adhesive spray and adhere two pieces together, shiny sides out. Score with stylus and fold in half to create 6½" x 5" top-fold card.

2. Cut 6½" x 5" piece of glossy white cardstock. Spray this piece with blue, green, and purple stained glass sheer color paint starting with green in upper left corner, blue in center, and purple in lower right-hand corner. Colors should overlap, blending gently into each other; let dry.

3. When paint is completely dry, cut 3½" x 2" rectangle out of center of painted cardstock using craft knife.

4. Spray back of painted cardstock with adhesive spray and adhere to front of card, over purple glossy cardstock.

5. Using craft knife, cut 3½" x 2" rectangle out of both metallic paper and glossy purple cardstock.

6. Edge all sides of card, inside rectangle, and outside edges with leafing pen.

Creating the star:

1. Cut one 4" x 3" piece of off-white cardstock. Spray front with adhesive spray. Immediately apply metallic leafing to completely cover cardstock. Brush away excess leafing. Repeat steps on back of cardstock.

2. Emboss cardstock with leafing using star embossing plate.

3. Cut out star. Adhere to card front towards left of opening by placing craft glue on star points that overlap edges of open rectangle; let dry.

Adding wire embellishments:

1. Cut 2" length of wire. Cut three 9" lengths of wire. Gently bend all 9" wires with needle-nose pliers to create swirls and waves at both ends.

2. Add beads to wires. Bend ends of wires to prevent beads from slipping off wire.

3. Bring wires together about 3" from end and wrap group of wires with 2" length of wire to hold them together.

4. With short end of wires to inside of card and long ends of wires to outside, adhere wire to back of star with craft glue; let dry.

Finishing the card:

1. Using gel pen, write "dream" on card front.

2. Cut 5½" x 1" strip of off-white cardstock and paint edges with leafing pen.

3. Using adhesive spray, adhere to bottom of inside of card making sure it doesn't show through card front opening.

4. Add journaling using gel pen *(photo A)*.

Friendship is the only CEMENT that will ever HOLD the world TOGETHER.

Woodrow Wilson

Love Be a Friend

Follow

Wish

FRIEND

Collage Tag

INSTRUCTIONS

1. Die-cut tag from poster board. Spray tag with interior-exterior paint; let dry. (This will provide a smooth surface for applying other paints and papers.) Spray other side of tag with same paint; let dry.

2. Spray back of tag with magnetic paint, covering thoroughly. Repeat 2-3 times; let dry thoroughly between each coat *(photo A)*.

3. Spray slide mount with satin spray paint; let dry.

4. Spray front of tag with adhesive spray. Tear and apply scrapbook papers in any desired fashion *(photo B)*. **Note:** Adhesive spray can also be sprayed onto backside of torn papers before applying.

5. After papers are applied, spray tag with matte finish spray; let dry. When dry, embellish as desired, using craft glue to adhere all embellishments. Paint all edges of tag with leafing pen.

6. Apply letter stickers to spell out desired message.

7. Add fiber trim through hole of tag.

Materials

- Adhesive spray
- Craft glue
- Die cut: jumbo tag
- Die-cut machine
- Embellishments: buttons, foam letters, quotes, ribbon
- Fiber trim
- Interior-exterior spray paint: ultra-flat white
- Leafing pen: gold
- Magnetic spray paint
- Matte finish spray
- Poster board
- Satin spray paint: cameo white
- Scrapbook paper: assorted patterns
- Slide mount: cardboard
- Stickers: bugs, flowers, letters

Make It Magnetic

Magnetic spray paint can be used on most any surface including glass, ceramic, metal, papier mâché, plaster, and wood. It creates a surface that magnets can stick to like the back of the Collage Tag. After applying the magnetic paint, you can topcoat the surface of your project so all of the elements match in color and style.

Spray paint and decoupage techniques were used to create the Collage Tag.

Give a Man
a Fish Tag

INSTRUCTIONS

1. Cut 3" x 5¼" piece of corrugated cardboard. (This is the tag.)
2. Peel back top layer of paper on cardboard, exposing corrugation on bottom right-hand corner and across bottom of tag as shown.
3. Tear 2" strip of drywall tape, peel away backing, and adhere to tag.

Materials

- Acid-free spray
- Adhesive spray
- Antiquing spray
- Burlap
- Cardstock: black, natural corrugated cardboard, off-white
- Chalk inks: blues, gray, yellow
- Craft glue
- Drywall tape: ¾" wide
- Fishing lure
- Glue dots
- Hemp twine
- Inkpad: black
- Iridescent spray
- Matte finish spray
- Quote: fishing-theme
- Rubber stamp: trout
- Ruler
- Scissors
- Stapler
- Staples: color of your choice
- Sticker: tape measure
- Webbing texture spray: black

Corrugated cardstock lends a rustic look to the Give a Man a Fish Tag.

4. Cut out and adhere quote to front of tag using adhesive spray.
5. Add tape measure sticker to lower front of tag, wrapping ends to back.
6. Spray tag with antiquing spray; let dry.
7. Stamp trout on top of tag.
8. Stamp trout on scrap piece of off-white cardstock, color in with chalk inks, and cut out shape. Spray trout shape with iridescent spray and adhere just above tape measure sticker on tag using craft glue.
9. Spray fishing lure with antiquing spray; let dry.
10. Cut 1" x 3" strip of burlap, fold in half, and staple to top of tag.
11. Wrap tag with hemp twine, dangling lure from twine.
12. Secure placement of lure with glue dot.
13. Spray tag with webbing texture; let dry.
14. Cut 3" x 5¼" piece of black cardstock. Adhere to back of tag using adhesive spray.
15. Spray tag with acid-free spray; let dry.
16. Spray tag with matte finish; let dry.

Luggage Tag

INSTRUCTIONS

1. Cut 2½" x 3" and 3¼" x 4" pieces of mat board.

2. Spray webbing texture all over 3¼" x 4" piece of mat board; let dry.

3. Using computer and printer, print name and address on one piece of scrapbook paper; trim to 2¼" x 2¾". Adhere to front of 3¼" x 4" piece of mat board with adhesive spray.

4. On another piece of scrapbook paper, print "If found, please call me" and phone number. Trim to size with decorative-edge scissors. Adhere to back of 2½" x 3" piece of mat board using adhesive spray (photo A).

5. On front of smaller piece of mat board, write initial with 18KT. gold leafing pen.

6. Paint all edges and sides of boards using leafing pen, using line of decorative-edged scissors as a guide.

7. Place smaller board on top of larger board. With pencil, mark where holes should be punched. Punch holes in tag.

8. Spray tag with digital photo and paper protectant spray; let dry.

9. Cut 15" length of ribbon and thread through slits in tag.

Materials

- Adhesive spray
- Computer and printer
- Digital photo and paper protectant spray
- Leafing pen: 18KT. gold
- Mat board: white
- Paper punch: small rectangular
- Pencil
- Ribbon: wired, ½" wide
- Scissors: decorative edge, straight edge
- Scrapbook paper: patterned (2)
- Webbing texture spray: white whisper

Gold webbing texture and a gold leafing pen were used on the Luggage Tag and work together to frame the initial on the front of the tag.

Cadet Jessica Hull
US Coast Guard Academy
7470 Chase Hall
New London, CT 06320

If found, please call me
705.689.3507

A

What makes this tag especially unique is the fact that it unbuckles and opens to show a hidden sewing kit.

Sewing Themed Tag

INSTRUCTIONS

1. Cut tag from cardstock; crease at fold lines *(see template)*.

2. Spray entire tag with antiquing spray; let dry.

3. Adhere pattern tissue to front, back, and inside of tag using adhesive spray.

4. Using brown chalk ink, stamp frayed fabric image randomly onto tag.

5. Using black inkpad, stamp sewing-themed images onto tag.

6. Paint edges of tag front and back with leafing pens, first with red shimmer then copper; let dry.

To finish inside of tag:

1. Cut 2½" x 4½" piece of off-white cardstock. Ink edges with brown ink and punch half circles into lower 1/3 of piece, two on each side directly across from each other. Wrap thread around cardstock as shown.

2. Tie thread through holes of five buttons and adhere to 2½" x 4½" piece off-white cardstock above wrapped thread. Stick threaded needle through cardstock next to buttons. Using felt-tip pen, draw stitch marks around edges.

3. Adhere embellished cardstock piece to inside of tag using adhesive spray.

4. Stamp ruler image onto balsa wood. Wrap ends of balsa wood with thread. Ink edges of balsa wood with brown chalk ink. Adhere stamped balsa wood

Materials

- Adhesive spray
- Antiquing spray
- Balsa wood: 1" x 3¼"
- Belt buckle: miniature
- Brad
- Cardstock: off-white
- Chalk ink: brown
- Double-sided tape
- Embellishments: buttons, miniature clothespin, needle, thread
- Felt-tip pen: fine-tip black
- Glue dots: mini
- Inkpad: black
- Leafing pens: copper, shimmering red
- Paper punch: circle
- Ribbon: blue and white striped, ⅓" wide
- Rubber stamps: dress form, frayed fabric, needle, ruler, sewing themed
- Ruler
- Scissors
- Tissue paper sewing pattern

piece across top of embellished cardstock piece using double-sided tape.

To finish front of tag:

1. Stamp dress form and needle package images onto off-white cardstock.

2. Ink images and cut out. Arrange on front of tag and adhere using double-sided tape.

To complete tag:

1. Spray ribbon with antiquing spray; let dry. Cut 5" length for top of tag and 10" length for "belt."

2. Paint belt buckle and brad with copper leafing pen; let dry.

3. Thread buckle onto one end of ribbon, secure with mini glue dot. Secure ribbon to back of tag using double-sided tape. Wrap ribbon around tag and loop through buckle to close.

4. Fold 5" piece of ribbon in half lengthwise. Place ribbon at top of tag as shown. Adhere to tag with brad.

5. Add miniature clothespin to tag.

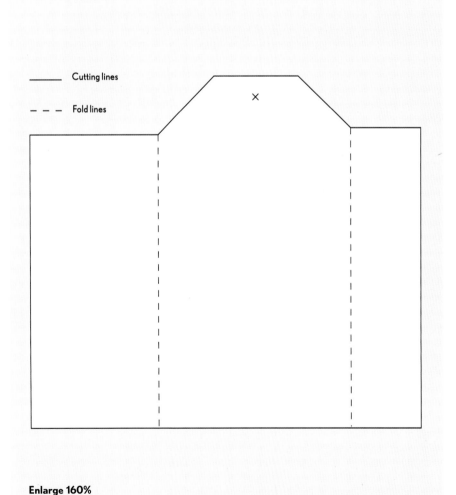

——— Cutting lines

– – – Fold lines

×

Enlarge 160%

Chapter 5

ALTERED ART

Making something new from something old is not a new art form, but it has certainly grabbed our attention as an artistic endeavor to be pursued. Altered art projects provide a place for you to "color outside the lines." Use these projects as a starting point and let your own creative style shine. Altered art is a very broad term, but in this chapter we focus on recreating purses, boxes, and clipboards.

Using basic spray paint and paper crafting techniques, you will learn to transform a metal lunch box into a retro-inspired purse and change a cigar box into a travel purse. Die cuts and gold texture paints turn an ordinary box into an extraordinary mosaic handbag.

Cardboard ornament box sets become memento and advent boxes, while a simple wood box is embellished to honor a special couple. Plain office clipboards are reborn into beautiful message centers using dimensional paint and paper techniques.

You also will learn how to make a heartfelt box perfect to store love letters and other treasures, and turn a book into an elegant clutch purse—complete with lining.

The level of difficulty of projects in this chapter ranges from simple to intermediate, but none require trade skills. You will want to set aside a bit of time to complete these projects, but they are well worth the time and effort.

Altered Clutch Purse

INSTRUCTIONS

To create outside of purse:

1. Gut hardcover book of all its pages by carefully cutting binding of pages with craft knife. Be very careful not to cut into book cover itself. **Note:** The binding will be the bottom of your purse and the book front and back will be the sides.

2. Using collection of scrapbook paper with vintage images, collage front and back of book

with torn and cut papers that have been sprayed with adhesive spray. Consider overlapping collage elements around edges of book cover to add interest (photo A).

3. Spray book with antiquing spray; let dry.

4. Stamp several postmarks on book cover collage.

5. Using screw punch, make hole in center of book about 1" from top on both front and back.

6. Lay book flat, collage side up, and spray with varnish; let dry. Repeat with second coat; let dry.

Who could imagine a purse from a book? If you prefer a larger or smaller purse, choose a smaller or larger book.

Materials

- Adhesive spray
- Antiquing spray
- Book: hardcover, at least 1" thick
- Book knob with screw: small
- Bookbinding tape: red, ¼"
- Chipboard
- Craft knife
- Elastic hair band: black
- Inkpad: black
- Rubber stamp: postmark
- Ruler
- Scissors
- Scrapbook paper: coordinating vintage image patterns, fabric-finish vintage letter patterned, fabric-finish envelope patterned, 12" x 12", as many as desired to complete project
- Screw punch
- Spray varnish

To create inside of purse:

1. Measure inside of cover excluding binding area. Cut two pieces of vintage letter paper in that size, one for back and one for front. Spray back of paper with adhesive spray and adhere to inside of cover.

2. Measure binding area of book (long, skinny rectangle). Cut piece of chipboard to that size. Cut piece of vintage letter paper ¼" bigger than chipboard. Spray back of paper with adhesive spray and cover chipboard with letter paper, tucking all raw edges to back side.

3. To create pleated sides of purse, modify template to fit measurements of purse *(see Template A)*. Expand bottom of triangle to match width of binding. Decide how wide you'd like book to open and expand top of triangle to match that size. You also need to consider how far up the side of the purse you'd like pleated insert to extend; adjust template accordingly. Cut two of inserts and two of linings *(see Template B)* from your customized template using vintage envelopes paper. Adhere lining to insert, wrong sides together, using adhesive spray. Crease

flaps towards lined side of insert. Crease pleat in insert by folding in half towards lining *(photo B)*.

4. Using red bookbinding tape, adhere insert's flaps to binding area. Continue taping up sides to front and back of purse, close to outside edge.

5. Spray wrong side of purse inserts with adhesive spray and adhere to inside of purse, covering flaps of inserts.

6. Press covered chipboard rectangle into bottom of purse to finish inside *(photo C)*.

Template A

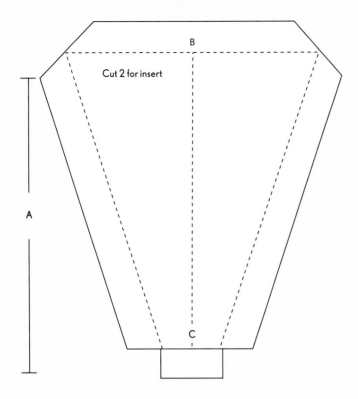

Cutting lines
Crease lines

B

Cut 2 for insert

A

C

D

To add the closure:

1. Push book knob into hole on front of book and secure with screw.

2. Thread elastic hair band through back hole and back through center of band to secure. Place loop over knob to close purse *(photo D)*.

Helpful Hints

Purse Perfection

• Consider making this purse from a very wide hardcover book if you would like it to stand on its own.

• You can purchase used books at library book sales, yard sales, and thrift stores.

• Add a handle to your purse. A decorative drawer pull or knob would work well and can be found at hardware and home improvement stores. Book knobs can be found at crafts and scrapbooking stores.

Template B

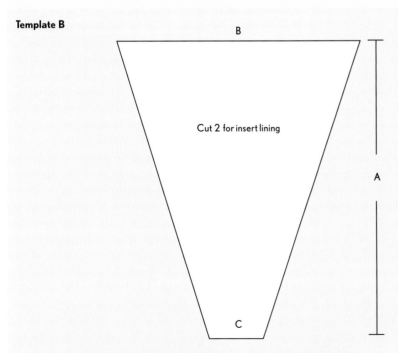

B

Cut 2 for insert lining

A

C

Enlarge 175%. Make modifications to fit your book. See Step 3.

Travel Purse

INSTRUCTIONS

To prep and paint box:

1. Using screwdriver, remove hinges, clasp, and handle; set aside.

2. Sand entire box and lid; wipe clean with soft cloth.

3. Spray three coats of primer on entire box and lid; let dry thoroughly after each coat. After last coat is dry, sand smooth; wipe clean with soft cloth.

4. Spray two coats of equestrian interior-exterior paint on inside of box and lid including top edges; let dry thoroughly after each coat.

5. Lay box and lid upside down. Spray two coats of woven tapestry interior-exterior paint on outside of box and lid; let dry thoroughly after each coat.

6. Spray one light coat of paint styling spray on one side of lid; immediately spray light coat of equestrian interior-exterior paint over paint styling spray; let dry.

Materials

- Adhesive spray
- Craft glue
- Gel stain: medium brown
- Interior-exterior spray paint: equestrian, woven tapestry
- Leafing pen: pale gold
- Paint styling spray
- Ruler
- Sandpaper
- Satin finish spray
- Scissors
- Scrapbook paper: faux crackle with words
- Screwdriver
- Soft cloth
- Spray primer: white
- Stickers: travel-themed
- Wood purse box with handle
- Wood signs: 1½" x 2¼" (3)

Travel images and a bamboo handle were used to embellish this cigar purse. You can use photographs and other memorabilia from a favorite vacation to embellish your own purse.

7. Repeat steps for remaining sides and top of lid; let dry.

8. Repeat steps for back of box; let dry.

To embellish front of purse:

1. Cut 7" x 8½" piece of scrapbook paper. Tear all edges.

2. Using gel stain and damp soft cloth, rub stain over torn edges and slightly in from torn edges. Sand random areas of paper to distress. Spray back of paper with adhesive spray, center on top of lid, and adhere to purse.

To cover wood signs:

1. Center and adhere sticker onto each wood sign. Using scissors, trim excess sticker if needed.

2. Using leafing pen, paint sides of wood signs and create narrow borders around stickers; let dry. Adhere signs to front of purse as shown using craft glue; let dry. Adhere stickers as desired. Sand stickers to distress as desired.

To embellish back of purse:

1. Adhere stickers as desired. Sand stickers to distress as desired.

2. Using leafing pen, paint outer edges on back of box; let dry *(photo A)*.

To finish purse:

1. Spray purse with two coats of satin finish spray.

2. Using screwdriver, re-attach hinges, clasp, and handle *(photo B)*.

A

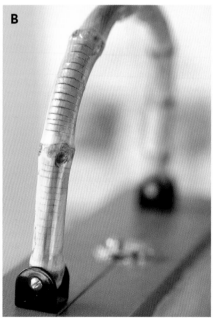

B

Helpful Hints

Unlimited Travel

This purse project can easily be adapted to your own travels. For instance, if your vacation was spent by the seashore, follow the instructions to prep the box, but paint the box blue. Add a layer of charcoal sand faux stone paint along the bottom for a sandy beach look, then embellish the purse with shells.

Mosaic Purse

INSTRUCTIONS

To create outside of box:

1. Remove lid from box. Spray outside of top and bottom of both pieces with faux suede paint; let dry. Apply another coat if needed; let dry.

2. Paint inside edges of box with leafing pen.

3. Spray two sheets of natural cardstock with faux stone paint; let dry.

4. Spray sheet of natural cardstock with metallic paint; let dry.

5. Using craft knife, slit one end of lid to make flap. Cut sections opposite flap at angle (see Diagram A, page 87).

6. Place lid on box bottom. Lay hinges where desired. Mark holes with pencil. Using piercing tool, make holes for paper fasteners; if holes are not large enough, use a nail to make holes slightly larger. Attach hinges with paper fasteners.

7. Die-cut desired star and mosaic shapes from painted cardstock (photo A). Brush craft glue onto pieces and place on box.

To add handle:

Note: Placement of handle can vary.

1. String wood beads onto desired length of wire.

2. Spray beads with flat black interior-exterior paint; let dry. Spray another coat if needed; let dry.

3. With piercing tool, make holes in box for wire, two on each side. Push wire through one hole and back through other. Twist wire 2-3 times at base of beads; cut wire. Repeat for other side of handle (photo B).

Materials

- Adhesive spray
- Beads: wood
- Button
- Cardstock: natural, 12"x 12" (3)
- Craft glue
- Craft knife
- Craft wire: 18-gauge
- Die cuts: circles, hearts
- Die-cut machine
- Elastic cording: black
- Embellishments: buttons, jewels, rhinestones
- Faux stone spray paint: metallic antique gold
- Faux suede spray paint: buckskin
- Hinges: brass (2)
- Interior-exterior spray paint: flat black
- Leafing pen: 18KT. gold
- Matte finish spray
- Metallic spray paint: 18KT. gold
- Needle-nose pliers
- Paintbrush: small
- Paper fasteners (8)
- Paper trimmer
- Papier-mâché box: 6-sided
- Pencil
- Piercing tool
- Scissors
- Scrapbook paper: your choice, as much as needed to cover inside of box

Any die-cut pattern can be used to create the Mosaic Purse. This stunning piece was painted in gold and embellished with black accents.

To add the closure:

1. Using piercing tool, make two holes in top of box for button closure. Thread desired length of elastic cording through shank of button. Push ends of elastic through holes; knot and dab with glue to secure knot.

2. Using piercing tool, make two holes in front lid edge for elastic loop. Cut length of elastic cording for loop. Push the ends of elastic cording through holes. Tie ends on inside and dab with glue to secure *(photo C)*. **Optional:** Cut three lengths of elastic cording;

vary colors if desired. Tie one end to form a knot and braid the three lengths, then tie another knot.

To finish box:

1. Add other embellishments to outside of box such as jewels or buttons *(photo D)*.

2. Spray inside of box with adhesive spray. Cut or tear pieces of scrapbook paper to cover inside of box.

3. Seal with two coats of matte finish spray; let dry thoroughly after each coat.

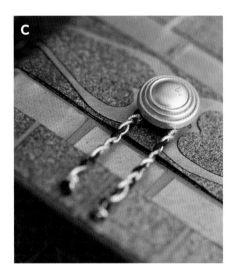

Diagram A

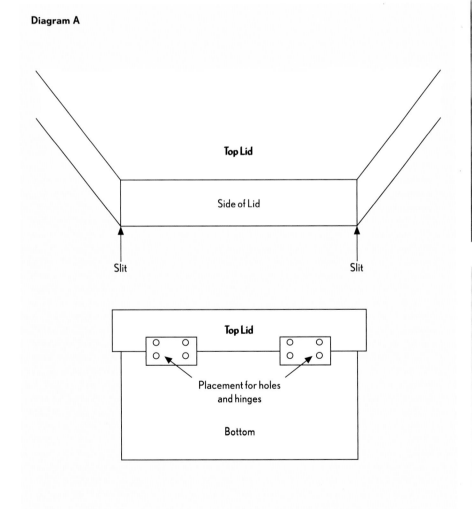

Top Lid

Side of Lid

Slit

Slit

Top Lid

Placement for holes and hinges

Bottom

Helpful Hints

Mosaic Options

When working on the mosaic purse project, it is helpful to refer to the photograph for placement of hinges, handle, and closure. Keep in mind that any mosaic design can be used. It is not necessary to use special die cuts for this project. The purse would look just as stunning if created using circle, square, or star die cuts.

Lunch Box Purse

INSTRUCTIONS

1. Close lunch box and shut clasp. Sand outside of lunch box to roughen surface; wipe clean with soft cloth.

2. Using painter's masking tape, mask off handle and clasp. Using craft knife, trim excess tape around handle hardware and clasp.

3. Spray three coats of primer on outside of lunch box; let dry between coats.

4. When dry, spray two coats of spray paint on outside of lunch box; let dry between coats.

5. When dry, use leafing pens to draw lines on tops of rims. Alternate colors and draw lines spaced evenly apart around front and back rims; let dry.

6. Using leafing pens, draw dots on sides of rims. Space dots evenly apart around sides of front and back rims. Use silver leafing pen for front and gold leafing pen for back.

7. Cut desired quotes and ephemera pieces from scrapbook papers.

8. Collage front of lunch box. Using adhesive spray, spray back of desired ephemera pieces. Position pieces on box, then smooth down.

9. Trim excess graphics from desired butterfly stickers. Remove backing, position over ephemera pieces, and smooth down.

10. Collage back of lunch box. Repeat steps for front of lunch box but use only butterfly stickers and quotes (photo A).

11. Collage sides of lunch box. Remove backing from thin decorative border sticker. Center one end of sticker on side by handle hardware.

Materials

- Adhesive spray
- Craft knife
- Leafing pens: 18KT. gold, silver
- Metal lunch box
- Painter's masking tape
- Sandpaper
- Satin finish spray
- Scissors
- Scrapbook paper: quotes, vintage ephemera
- Soft cloth
- Spray paint: mimosa
- Spray primer: white
- Stickers: butterflies, thin decorative border

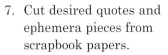

Start with a vintage lunch box or a new one to create this darling butterfly purse.

Whereso ever you go, go with all your heart.

Gratitude is the heart's memory.

Wrap sticker around side and smooth down *(photo B)*. Repeat steps for other side. Where two pieces meet on back, trim excess and overlap slightly in middle. Place small piece of decorative border sticker between handle *(photo C)*.

12. Trim excess graphics from desired butterfly stickers. Remove backing and center one butterfly on each side over decorative border sticker and smooth down. Using craft knife, cut stickers along ridges where rims meet box. Remove

those portions of stickers and reposition just above and below ridges *(photo D)*.

13. Spray two light coats of satin finish on outside of lunch box; let dry. Remove masking tape from handle and clasp.

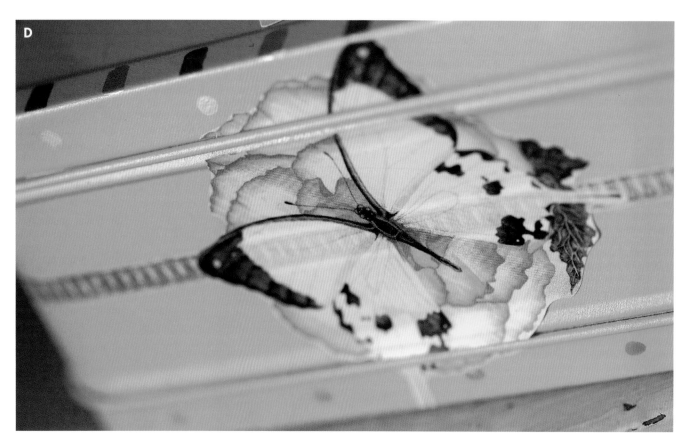

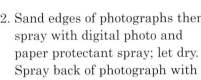

Johnson and Johnson Box

INSTRUCTIONS

To decorate outside of box:

1. Spray inside and outside of box with two coats of bordeaux faux suede paint; let dry after each coat.

2. Spray inside and outside of box with two coats of matte finish spray; let dry after each coat.

3. Spray chipboard letters with buckskin faux suede paint; let dry. Spray back of chipboard letters with adhesive spray and adhere to front of box.

4. Spray back of wallpaper cutout with adhesive spray and adhere to front of box.

5. Attach button to front of box with large glue dot (photo A).

To decorate inside of box:

1. Cut two 7¾" square pieces of off-white cardstock. Spray both pieces with two coats of bordeaux faux suede paint; let dry after each coat. (These are the inside pages.)

2. Sand edges of photographs then spray with digital photo and paper protectant spray; let dry. Spray back of photograph with adhesive spray and adhere to inside pages as desired.

3. Ink edges of scrapbook quotes, scrapbook definitions, and other ephemera with brown ink; let dry.

4. Cut 3¼" x 5½" piece of cardstock. Align desired chipboard letters on piece of cardstock and spray with buckskin faux suede paint; let dry.

5. Remove chipboard letters from top of cardstock.

6. Spray back of cardstock with adhesive spray and adhere to inside page that will go on right side of box as shown.

7. Affix painted chipboard letters to inside page that will go on left side of box as shown using small glue dots.

8. Using brads and stapler, scrapbook definitions, scrapbook

Materials

- Adhesive spray
- Brads: small
- Button
- Cardstock: off-white, 8½"x 11" (3)
- Chipboard letters
- Digital photo and paper protectant spray
- Ephemera
- Faux suede spray paint: bordeaux, buckskin
- Glue dots: large, small
- Inkpad: brown
- Matte finish spray
- Metal word tags
- Photographs: desired sizes (2)
- Ruler
- Sandpaper
- Scissors
- Scrapbook definitions
- Scrapbook quotes
- Stapler
- Wallpaper cutout: desired scene
- Wood box with hinges and clasp: 8¼"x 8¼"x 1¾"

quotes, and metal word tags, embellish both inside pages as desired.

9. Spray back of each inside page with adhesive spray. Adhere one page onto each side of box interior.

The inside of the Johnson and Johnson Box holds two "scrapbook" pages that were cut to size, embellished, and then adhered to the box.

Heartfelt Nostalgia Box

INSTRUCTIONS

1. Paint entire outside of box and lid with gesso spray; let dry.

2. Cut suede scrapbook paper to fit inside of box, lid, and bottom outside of box. Affix using adhesive spray.

3. Paint edges of box with leafing pen.

4. Spray shelf paper with metallic paint; let dry. Wad up paper into small ball. Open paper up, then wad into ball once again. Repeat this process several times until paper has wrinkles and cracks all over its surface.

5. Soak shelf paper in water until it relaxes and lays flat; let dry.

6. Tear shelf paper into irregular pieces and adhere pieces onto entire outside of box and lid using craft glue; let dry.

7. When glue has dried thoroughly, spray sponge with antiquing spray and apply to surface of box and lid.

8. Using clean sponge, apply glaze to surface of box and lid; let dry. When glaze has soaked into cracks of paper, gently remove excess color with paper towel.

9. Lightly burnish paper with paper towel.

10. Edge bottom of box with two rows of pearl strings. Attach beaded fringe to edges of lid using craft glue; let dry *(photo A)*.

11. Attach lace to top of lid using adhesive spray.

12. Arrange vintage postcards on lid and adhere using adhesive spray.

13. Spray photograph with digital photo and paper protectant spray; let dry. Paint edges of photograph and photo corners with leafing pen.

Materials

- Adhesive spray
- Antiquing spray
- Beaded fringe
- Craft glaze: taupe
- Craft glue
- Craft sponges (2)
- Digital photo and paper protectant spray
- Embellishments: appliqué flowers, dried flowers, heart locket charm, lace, tiny pearls
- Gesso spray
- Leafing pen: gold
- Metallic spray paint: gold
- Paper towels
- Papier-mâché box: heart-shape
- Pearl strings: 2.5mm, 4mm (2 ft. each)
- Photo corners (4)
- Photograph: desired size
- Ribbon: gold grosgrain, ½" wide
- Scissors
- Scrapbook paper: deep red suede
- Self-adhesive shelf paper: white
- Tassel: gold
- Vintage postcards: reduced to fit

A

Our nostalgic heart box is the perfect place to store old love letters and memorabilia.

14. Attach photo corners to top of lid and add photograph.

15. Tie 3" length of grosgrain ribbon to heart locket. Attach tassel by hiding string underneath gold ribbon.

16. Attach ribbon at center top of lid using craft glue. **Note:** This will allow tassel to dangle at center back of box *(photo B)*.

17. Arrange flower appliqués and dried flowers on box lid. Adhere using adhesive spray. Add tiny pearls as desired *(photo C)*.

Memento Boxes

INSTRUCTIONS

1. Spray photographs with digital photo and paper protectant spray; let dry.

2. Untie and remove all gold cording from small boxes; set cords aside.

3. Spray light random coat of primer on all boxes and lids; let dry.

4. Spray light random coat of metallic spray paint on all boxes and lids; let dry.

5. Spray light random coat of antiquing spray on all boxes and lids; let dry.

6. Spray light random coat of whitewash on all boxes and lids; let dry.

7. Embellish small lids as desired; adhere photographs and papers to fit small box lids with paint-brush and one coat of decoupage medium *(photo A)*. Smooth down with fingers then with brayer.

8. Apply three additional coats of decoupage medium; let dry thoroughly after each coat.

9. Embellish large lid as desired. Cut background paper to cover lid, leaving border of box.

Materials

- Antiquing spray
- Brayer
- Craft glue
- Decoupage medium
- Digital photo and paper protectant spray
- Embellishments: clock face, typewriter key stickers, vellum die cuts
- Key: old-fashioned
- Metallic spray paint: brushed nickel
- Paintbrush: 1"
- Papier-mâché box: rectangle set with 24 box ornaments
- Pencil
- Photographs (to embellish top of large and small box tops)
- Picture frame: small
- Scissors
- Scrapbook paper: theme of your choice; as many as needed to achieve desired look
- Spray bottle with water
- Spray primer: gray
- Whitewash spray

This pretty box opens to reveal a set of memento boxes embellished with layers of paints and images and packed full of memories.

HOME

Distress papers by spraying with water, wrinkling, smoothing out, then tearing edges; let dry. Spray light, random coats of antiquing and whitewash on distressed papers; let dry.

10. Using paintbrush, apply one coat of decoupage medium to back of paper and top of lid. Center paper on top of lid, smooth down with fingers and brayer.

11. Spray light coat of whitewash on picture frame; let dry.

12. Cut desired image from scrapbook paper.

13. Cut photograph to fit inside picture frame.

14. Arrange image, photograph, frame, and key on top of lid. Once desired placement is achieved, remove frame and key. Mark placement of image and photograph with light pencil lines. Remove image and photograph. Using paintbrush, apply one coat of decoupage medium on back of image and photograph and reposition on top of lid within pencil lines. Apply three additional coats of decoupage medium over entire lid; let dry thoroughly after each coat.

15. Using craft glue, run bead on back of frame and place over photograph; let dry.

16. Apply glue to backside of key and secure to lid; let dry.

17. Spell out desired word under frame using typewriter key stickers (photo B).

18. Re-thread gold cords into small boxes and lids and tie knots; trim excess cord.

19. Re-pack small boxes into large box.

Celebrate Special Days

Memento boxes can be embellished to mark any occasion. Create a set for a new mother and embellish small boxes with "first tooth," "first lock of hair," etc. The set of boxes also could be decorated with photographs, invitations, or tickets to remember a special vacation or birthday.

These boxes were embellished to celebrate Christmas. Instead of a store-bought Advent calendar, create your own that little ones can open throughout the holiday season. Metallic marbled paper dresses up the look of the boxes, making these ready for display.

Telephone Center Altered Clipboard

INSTRUCTIONS

To make clipboard base:

1. Lightly sand surface of clipboard. (Remove any labels or stickers first.)

2. Spray clipboard with metallic paint; let dry. Repeat if necessary.

3. Spray clipboard with antiquing spray; let dry. **Note:** Allowing uneven coverage will add an aged and worn appearance.

4. Using black inkpad, stamp clipboard with harlequin and script stamps. Wipe off ink with soft cloth (this will lift the antiquing spray in the stamped image).

5. Using black ink, stamp edges of clipboard; let dry.

6. Spray light coat of webbing texture over surface of clipboard.

7. Tear 8" x 10½" rectangle from script scrapbook paper. (Save scraps for decorating pencil.) Ink torn edges with chalk ink. Spray back of paper with adhesive spray. Center paper and adhere to clipboard. Spray clipboard with matte finish.

To make telephone numbers flipchart:

1. Cut 7¼" x 10½" piece of off-white cardstock. Fold in half to 5¼" x 7¼" rectangle. (This is the cover of flipchart.)

2. Cut four 5¾" x 7" rectangles from off-white cardstock. (These will be the pages in the flipchart.)

Materials

- Adhesive spray
- Antiquing spray
- Cardstock: off-white, 8½" x 11" (5)
- Chalk ink: brown
- Clipboard: letter size
- Computer and printer
- Corkboard: ¼" thick, 4" x 4"
- Craft glue
- Craft knife
- Double-sided tape
- Fiber trim: assorted earth tones
- Inkpad: black
- Leafing pen: 18KT. gold
- Masking tape
- Matte finish spray
- Metallic spray paint: 18KT. gold
- Pushpins: round head
- Rubber stamps: harlequin, script
- Ruler
- Sandpaper
- Scissors
- Scrapbook paper: gold check, script, tiles with da Vinci theme, 12" x 12"
- Self-adhesive hook-and-loop tape: black
- Self-stick note pad: 1⅜" x 1⅞"
- Shipping tag: large
- Soft cloth
- Stylus
- Tags: metal-rimmed, round (2)
- Vellum: off-white, 8½" x 11"
- Webbing texture spray: gold
- Wood pencil

Place the Telephone Center Altered Clipboard next to the phone and everything you need is right at your fingertips.

3. On bottom ⅝" of each page, cut 2" tabs that slightly overlap, allowing all four tabs to be visible. First tab begins ¼" from lower left edge; second tab begins 1¾" from left edge; third tab begins 3¼" from left edge; forth tab begins 4¾" from left edge. Ink edges and surfaces of all pages with chalk ink.

4. Using black ink, stamp tabs with script stamp.

5. Layer pages and tuck into cover.

6. Tear 5⅛" x 7⅛" piece of gold check scrapbook paper. Spray back of paper with adhesive spray and adhere to cover of flipchart.

7. Cut 2" x 6¾" strip of tiles scrapbook paper. Spray back of strip with adhesive spray and adhere across bottom of flipchart cover.

8. Using computer and printer, print in brown ink "Telephone Numbers" on piece of vellum about 4" from top of page. Near bottom of vellum page,

in brown ink, print in smaller font "Family," "Friends," "Business," and "Emergency."

9. From printed sheet of vellum, cut 6" x 6½" rectangle with "Telephone Numbers" about 4" from top. Tear all sides to achieve uneven edges. Fold ½" of top of vellum over top of cover. Spray back 6" x 6½" rectangle of vellum with adhesive spray and adhere over printed papers on cover.

10. Tear each of four words printed at bottom of vellum into rectangles measuring 1¾" x ½". Spray back of each word with adhesive spray and adhere to tabs of pages.

11. Tuck flipchart under clip on clipboard.

To make mini bulletin board:

1. Using craft knife, cut corkboard into 4" square.

2. Using black ink, stamp script over surface of corkboard.

3. Using leafing pen, paint edges of corkboard.

4. Spray corkboard with matte finish.

5. Spray several pushpins with antiquing spray; let dry (photo A).

To make pencil holder:

1. Cut 3" x 4" rectangle from gold check scrapbook paper.

2. Fold edges in towards center, ¾" down each long side creating 1½" x 4" rectangle. Ink edges of rectangle with chalk ink.

3. Wrap rectangle around pencil to size a tube to hold pencil. Adhere ends together using double-sided tape. (This is the pencil holder.)

4. Adhere to back of corkboard with pencil holder extending above top.

5. Attach corkboard with pencil holder to lower right quarter of clipboard using craft glue; let dry. Add pushpins.

To make self-stick note pad holder:

1. Spray shipping tag with antiquing spray on both sides; let dry.

2. Using black ink, stamp with script stamp.

3. Paint edges of front and back of tag with leafing pen.

4. Using stylus, score tag from bottom at these measurements: ⅞", 1¼", 2⅞", 3½".

5. Fold at scored lines.

6. Tie fiber trim through hole in tag.

7. Cut ½" circle of self-adhesive hook-and-loop tape and adhere under flap as closure.

8. Peel away last sheet from self-stick pad and insert into holder.

9. Adhere to bottom left quarter of clipboard with craft glue *(photo B)*.

To make decorated pencil:

1. Mask off eraser end of wood pencil using masking tape.

2. Spray pencil with adhesive spray.

3. Using saved scraps from script paper, wrap pencil with 1¼"-wide rectangle measuring length of pencil. Spray wrapped pencil with antiquing spray; let dry.

4. Spray light coat of webbing texture onto wrapped pencil; let dry.

5. Remove masking tape.

6. Paint metal band on pencil with leafing pen; let dry.

7. Insert pencil into pencil holder.

To make dangling tags:

1. Cut four 2¼" circles from scrapbook paper.

2. Spray back of paper circles with adhesive spray and adhere images to front and back of metal-rimmed tags.

3. Attach tags to top of clipboard with fiber trim.

Finishing touches:

1. Cut additional tiles from scrapbook paper. Adhere to clipboard using adhesive spray.

2. Tie variety of fiber trims to clip on clipboard.

Helpful Hints

Tabs & Tearing

To achieve perfect looking tabs when creating the flipchart, trace around a domino. To help achieve torn edges, use a metal ruler as a guide when tearing papers.

Garden Notes
Altered Clipboard

INSTRUCTIONS

To make clipboard:

1. Lightly sand clipboard; wipe with soft cloth. Mask clip with masking tape.

2. Spray front and back of clipboard with gesso spray; let dry.

3. Paint clipboard with craft paint, allowing brush strokes to show texture; let dry. For additional texture, lay craft mesh on clipboard in random areas and apply chalk ink through mesh.

4. Remove masking tape from clip. Lightly spray clip and board with stained glass sheer color paint; let dry.

5. When dry, lightly sand edges and surface of clipboard to allow white of gesso to show through.

6. Cut 8" x 11" piece of scrapbook paper and tear edges. Ink edges with chalk ink.

7. Tear 3" x 11" strip of scrapbook paper. Ink edges with chalk ink. (This piece will create a pocket at bottom of clipboard.) Sew sides and bottom of strip to create pocket *(photo A)*.

8. Continue sewing around entire piece of paper.

9. Spray back of paper with adhesive spray and adhere to clipboard.

Materials

- Adhesive spray
- Cardstock: purple, 8½"x 11"
- Chalk ink: violet
- Clipboard: letter size
- Corkboard: ¼" thick, 4"x 4"
- Craft glue
- Craft mesh
- Craft paint: acid-free, brush-on, purple
- Die cuts: alphabet
- Die-cut machine
- Double-sided tape
- Embellishments: small paper flowers, small purple beads
- Flower seed packets (2)
- Gesso spray
- Glue dots
- Masking tape
- Matte finish spray
- Paintbrush: 1"
- Paper clips
- Ribbons: 2-3 coordinating colors
- Ruler
- Sandpaper
- Scissors
- Scrapbook paper: floral theme, 8½"x 11" (3)
- Self-stick note pad: 3"x 4"
- Sewing machine
- Soft cloth
- Stained glass sheer color spray paint: purple
- Swirl paper clips
- Wood pencil

A

What a handy tool for note taking, and fun to look at, too! The front pocket of the Garden Notes Altered Clipboard is a perfect place to store seed packets or catalog clippings.

To Do List
~ Plan Garden Plots
~ Buy flower seeds
~ Turn soil

COSMOS
200
MG

ASTER
Crego Mix
150
MG

Garden Notes

Noteworthy Gifts

You can customize clipboards to meet many of your needs. How about a shopping list board, a driving directions board, a gift list board... use your imagination! They're fun, easy to create, and make great gifts.

To make pencil holder:

1. Tear 2½" x 4" rectangle from scrapbook paper. Wrap rectangle around pencil and adhere edges where papers touch using double-sided tape.

2. Tuck pencil tube under right edge of paper as shown. Adhere with craft glue; let dry.

3. Lightly sand pencil. Wrap pencil with craft mesh. Spray with stained glass sheer color paint; let dry. Remove craft mesh.

4. Tie ribbon around end of pencil. Insert pencil into holder.

To make corkboard squares:

1. Cut three 2" squares from corkboard. Ink edges of squares with chalk ink; let dry.

2. Adhere to clipboard with craft glue; let dry *(photo B)*.

Finishing touches:

1. Adhere paper flowers and beads to corkboard squares using craft glue; let dry.

2. Die-cut "Garden Notes" from purple cardstock. Spray back of letters with adhesive spray and adhere to front of pocket.

3. Cut flower shape from scrapbook paper. Ink edges with chalk ink. Adhere to clip with glue dot *(photo C)*. Spray entire board with matte finish; let dry.

4. Cut several lengths of coordinating ribbons and tie through hole in clip.

5. Tear last page of self-stick notepad and adhere to board.

6. Sand edges of seed packets; tuck in pocket. Add swirl paperclips to edge of pocket.

WHEN SHADOWS FALL

THE LIGHT WILL SUSTAIN

Chapter 6

HOME ACCESSORIES

Beyond books, boxes, and purses, there is a growing trend in the altering of other items, including home décor accessories. When you think about it, just about anything can be altered. Found objects— from picture frames to candles—are ready canvases for this hugely popular art form.

Beautiful objects can best be enjoyed if they are useful. When choosing the objects you want to alter, think of how they can be used. Consider the story you want to tell, because more than any other craft, altered art can be used to share a personal anecdote. You can tell an account of family history or a tale of the person receiving a gift of an altered piece.

In this chapter you will learn how to dress up store-bought glass candles; use mirror paint to transform plain picture frames into tabletop art and trays; recall a story of family history on a recycled bottle; and embellish a coin frame with mementos of a loved one. You will also learn techniques to achieve special effects when using spray paints on these projects—from water spotting to applying crackle paints on paper.

Like most altered art, these projects require a bit more time to finish than a scrapbook page or card, yet they are so much fun to embellish.

Ponder Grace Candle

INSTRUCTIONS

1. Spray front of vellum with digital photo and digital photo and paper protectant spray; let dry.

2. Using script font in size 72 for both capital letters and size 36 for rest of letters, type "Ponder Grace" two times, once at upper right-hand corner of paper and once at lower left-hand corner of paper. Print sample and place under vellum.

3. Repeat until desired layout is achieved, then print words on vellum. Wrap vellum around candle and cut to fit with ¼" overlap.

4. Spray front of vellum with digital photo and digital photo and paper protectant spray; let dry.

5. Spray back edges of vellum with adhesive spray and adhere to candle, making sure to leave ¼" of glass at top.

6. Stuff candle opening with paper towels to keep inside glass free of paint. **Note:** Make sure towels are tucked completely inside.

7. Spray crackle basecoat on vellum, making sure not to paint over words and to leave random bits of vellum exposed. (Practice this step on a few sample pieces of printed paper. A little overspray is expected and desired near the words.) Paint glass lip at top of candle with a few quick passes; let dry.

8. Spray crackle topcoat over basecoat, again making sure not to paint over words, to achieve crackled effect; let dry. **Note:** Parts of the first coat will be exposed and is desired. Crackle will occur within a few minutes.

9. Spray vellum with gloss finish spray; let dry.

Materials

- Adhesive spray
- Computer and printer
- Digital photo and paper protectant spray
- Glass candle: white, 8½" tall
- Gloss finish spray
- Paper towels
- Ruler
- Scissors
- Spray crackle basecoat: metallic gold
- Spray crackle topcoat: buttercup
- Vellum: white, 8½"x 11"

Helpful Hints

Candle Safety

Here are a few safety tips to keep in mind when using your candles:

1. Extinguish all candles when leaving a room or going to sleep.

2. Keep candles away from items that can catch fire such as curtains, bedding, and clothing.

3. Keep candles away from flammable liquids.

4. Place candles on a steady surface to prevent tipping.

5. Keep candle wicks trimmed to ¼".

6. Candles in glass containers should be extinguished before the last ½" of wax starts to melt.

You Have Been Given Candle

INSTRUCTIONS

1. Spray front of vellum with digital photo and paper protectant spray; let dry. On scrap paper and with your favorite font, print "You have been Given." Wrap printed test paper around candle to determine placement of phrase. When satisfied, print words on vellum. Wrap vellum around candle and trim to fit candle with ¼" overlap at back. Spray front of vellum with digital photo and paper protectant spray.

2. Hold vellum between thumb and forefinger. At a distance of 16" to 18" depress paint nozzle slightly, painting stream into air. Move paper into path of paint stream; move can around edges of paper, creating top, bottom, and side borders with droplets; let dry. **Note:** Holding the can sideways is helpful for creating droplets.

3. Wrap vellum around glass; secure with glue dots.

4. Paint rim of candle with leafing pen.

5. Pick up crystals with tweezers; dip into glue. Place crystals down center of phrasing, from top to bottom.

6. Finish candle with accent piece of wire approximately 15" long. Thread large crystal bead onto wire. Pass one wire end through bead again, creating loop large enough to encircle candle snugly. Slide wire circle over candle, then add craft glue at bead back to hold in place. Create spiral twists at both wire ends.

7. Set candle on angel hair cloud. Drop pieces of craft thread randomly onto angel hair.

Materials

- Angel hair
- Computer and printer
- Craft glue
- Craft thread: gold, pink, silver
- Craft wire: 24-gauge, silver
- Crystal bead: large
- Crystals: flat-back, pink, clear, small (8-10 each)
- Digital photo and paper protectant spray
- Glass candle: white, 8½" tall,
- Glue dots
- Interior-exterior spray paint: glossy black
- Leafing pen: silver
- Needle-nose pliers
- Ruler
- Scissors
- Scrap paper: 8½"x 11"
- Tweezers
- Vellum: white, 8½"x 11"

Helpful Hints

Angel Hair Options

Traditional angel hair most often was white and made from spun glass fibers that could be irritating to hands. Today, glass fiber angel hair is softer to the touch.

Angel hair is also made from finely spun metal fibers that are available in a wide variety of colors. An Internet search will turn up many suppliers of this sometimes hard-to-find embellishment.

Prose Candle

INSTRUCTIONS

1. Spray vellum with digital photo and paper protectant spray; let dry. With computer, print onto vellum:
   Layaway in your Heart
   Ponder the Grace
   You have been
   Given
   Note: Print on paper first and place paper behind vellum to check placement of words. When satisfied, print on vellum.

2. Spray vellum with digital photo and paper protectant spray; let dry.

3. Wrap vellum around candle, making sure to center phrasing. Cut to fit candle with ¼" overlap at back. Cut transparency film slightly larger.

4. Spray printed vellum with antiquing spray, leaving word area virtually free of paint; let dry. Holding can of crackle topcoat 18" from vellum, spray over antiquing and very slightly over words; let dry. Spray one more coat of antiquing, then one more coat of crackle topcoat; let dry after each coat. **Note:** Take care to not cover words.

5. Flick small water droplets onto tray or clean counter surface. Lay vellum with painted and printed side face up onto water droplets; smooth paper. Lift moistened vellum and smooth onto dry, flat surface, creasing wrinkles; let dry.

6. Lay transparency smooth-side up over dry painted vellum. Draw chalk line around words showing through, creating frame effect on transparency. Lay transparency flat. Spray antique bronze paint in a mist around chalk lines; let dry.

7. Wrap vellum around candle and secure with glue dots. Overlap transparency at same place and secure with glue dots.

8. Tie trims with bow and streamer at right top and bottom left, keeping ribbon well below rim of candle.

Materials

- Antiquing spray
- Candle: white, 8½" tall
- Chalk: white
- Computer and printer
- Crackle topcoat: ballerina
- Digital photo and paper protectant spray
- Fiber trim or ribbon
- Glue dots
- Plastic tray
- Ruler
- Scissors
- Spray paint: antique bronze
- Transparency film: 8½"x 11"
- Vellum: pink, 8½"x 11"
- Water

Helpful Hints

Pretty Candles

Play with font sizes and styles to find what best suits your personality. Print out a few samples to see how they look wrapped around the candle. If you don't like what fonts you have, they can be found on the Internet—free or for purchase.

You also can add embellishments to the vellum. How about some pretty buttons or small vintage jewelry pieces? Adhere to the vellum with glue dots.

Vintage Shadow Box

INSTRUCTIONS

1. Sand entire box and ball knobs; wipe clean with soft cloth.

2. Using pencil, mark center in each corner on front edges of box. Pre-drill hole in each corner ¼" deep.

3. Spray two coats of primer over entire box and ball knobs, leaving flat sides of ball knobs unfinished; let dry after each under coat.

4. Sand box and wipe clean with soft cloth.

5. Using masking tape, mask off top, sides, and bottom of box. Spray two coats of parchment spray paint on inside and front edges of box; let dry after each coat. Remove masking tape.

6. Using masking tape, mask off front edges of box. Lay box face down. Spray three coats of metallic spray paint on outside of box and ball knobs, leaving flat sides of ball knobs unfinished; let dry after each coat.

7. Remove masking tape.

8. Spray two coats of satin finish over entire box and ball knobs, leaving flat sides of ball knobs unfinished; let dry after each under coat.

Using basic spray paint and paper-crafting techniques, a plain brown shadowbox is transformed into a treasure chest for tiny antiques and collectibles.

9. Add background paper. Using ruler and craft knife, measure and cut piece of desired scrapbook paper slightly smaller than inside back of box. Spray back of paper with adhesive spray. Align one edge of paper along one edge of inside back of box. Once aligned, smooth down remaining paper.

10. From same scrapbook paper, measure and cut four strips of paper to cover front edges of box. Spray back of strips with adhesive spray and adhere to front edges of box.

11. Cut out desired image from scrapbook paper to layer on top of background paper. Trim if necessary to fit inside of box. Spray back of image with adhesive spray and adhere to piece of white cardstock. Trim cardstock to size of image.

Materials

- Adhesive spray
- Ball knobs: 1¼" (4)
- Cardstock: white, 8½"x 11"
- Charms: silver
- Craft glue
- Craft knife
- Craft wire: 20-gauge
- Drill
- Drill bit: size of upholstery tacks
- Masking tape
- Metallic spray paint: charcoal
- Needle-nose pliers with wire cutter
- Pencil
- Ruler
- Sandpaper
- Satin finish spray
- Scissors
- Scrapbook paper: vintage ephemera
- Soft cloth
- Spray paint: parchment
- Spray primer: white
- Upholstery tacks (4)
- Wall box

A

Spray back of cardstock with adhesive spray and adhere to inside of box.

12. Cut three phrases from scrapbook paper. Spray back of phrases with adhesive spray and adhere inside and on top of box as desired *(photo A)*.

13. Turn box upside down. Using craft glue, run bead around unfinished flat sides of ball knobs. Place knobs in corners ¼" in from sides; let dry.

14. Lay box flat. Push upholstery tacks into pre-drilled holes.

15. Cut 30" length of craft wire. Starting from upper left upholstery tack, wind wire once around tack, leaving 1" tail. Thread desired charms onto wire before proceeding to next upholstery tack.

16. Continue to wind wire around remaining upholstery tacks ending at upper left corner.

17. Trim excess wire with wire cutter on pliers. Crimp ends of wire under upholstery tack using pliers.

18. Slide charms in place *(photo B)*.

19. Fill box with desired antiques and collectibles.

B

When Shadows Fall Box

INSTRUCTIONS

1. Copy vintage photograph onto one sheet of cardstock; trim to size.

2. Using computer and printer, print "When shadows fall" and "The light will sustain" on one sheet of cardstock. Trim sayings to fit frame as shown.

3. Edge photograph and sayings with leafing pen. With damp cloth, dab painted edges to lift some paint; let dry. Spray photograph and sayings with digital photo and paper protectant spray; let dry.

4. In plastic bowl, thin small amount of black paint (two parts paint, one part water) and stir. Place droplets of paint onto 8½" x 11" cardstock. Lay paper towel directly on top to achieve

Materials

- Adhesive spray
- Cardstock: glossy finish, white, 8½"x 11" (3)
- Computer and printer
- Craft foam: ½" thick, 5" square
- Craft glue
- Craft paint: acid-free, brush-on, black
- Craft thread: copper
- Digital photo and paper protectant spray
- Embellishments: crystals, glitter, rhinestones
- Glue dots
- Leafing pen: red shimmer
- Paintbrush: 1"
- Paper towel
- Photograph: vintage, 3½"x 5"
- Plastic bowl
- Ruler
- Satin finish spray paint: mimosa
- Scissors
- Shadow box: natural wood, 8"x 8"
- Silk flowers (2)
- Soft cloth
- Texture spray paint

A shallow shadow box serves as a pretty picture frame. Texture, color, and embellishments were used to finish the project.

WHEN SHADOWS FALL

THE LIGHT WILL SUSTAIN

"spilled ink effect" and to soak up excess black paint. Lift paper towel straight up to avoid rubbing; let dry. Cut cardstock to 5¾" square. (This is the background paper.)

5. Spray shadow box with texture spray paint; let dry. Texture becomes apparent as paint dries; let dry 24 hours. Repeat if desired for deeper texturing effects.

6. Spray inside and inner edge of shadow box with satin finish spray paint; let dry.

7. At outer edges of shadow box, spray satin finish spray paint over original textured spray paint. **Note**: If desired, let some textured spray paint show through.

8. Spatter droplets of satin finish spray paint onto background paper by depressing nozzle slightly and moving paper under spray; let dry.

9. Spray back of background paper with adhesive spray and adhere to shadow box as shown.

10. Cut piece of craft foam to 3" x 4". Adhere to center of background paper using craft glue; let dry.

11. Spray back of photograph with adhesive spray and adhere to center of craft foam.

12. Adhere phrases and flowers as shown using glue dots.

13. Using paintbrush, brush craft glue on background paper and edges of shadow box. Add rhinestones and glitter as desired; let dry.

14. Add craft thread around photograph and flowers as desired (photo A).

A

Store-bought items embellish the coin frame, but it would be equally charming dressed up with game pieces, shells, and tiny toys.

Materials

- Adhesive spray
- Cardboard coin holder
- Cardstock: red
- Computer and printer
- Digital photo and paper protectant spray
- Embellishments: bottle caps, buttons, charms, coins, miniature playing card, watch parts
- Faux suede spray paint: buckskin
- Inkpad: brown
- Photo corners: self-adhesive
- Photographs (4)
- Ribbon: black, black-and-white polka dot
- Rub-on letters
- Ruler
- Sandpaper
- Scissors
- Soft cloth
- Stickers: plastic, postal, timepieces
- Transparency film: 8½" x 11"

Coin Holder Frame

INSTRUCTIONS

1. Spray coin holder with faux suede spray paint; let dry.

2. Embellish coin holder as desired.

3. Sand edges of photographs; wipe with soft cloth. Spray photographs with digital photo and paper protectant spray; let dry.

4. Cut four pieces of red cardstock same size as each photograph. Ink edges of cardstock with brown ink; let dry.

5. Using computer and printer, journal as desired, making sure to fill page. Print out journaling on transparency.

6. Spray printed side of transparency with digital photo and paper protectant spray; let dry. Cut two pieces of transparency—one to cover right back side, the other to cover left back side of coin holder. Using adhesive spray, adhere pieces of transparency to front and back of coin holder.

7. Cut piece of red cardstock slightly larger than photograph to be used on right side of back of frame. Using adhesive spray, adhere cardstock to transparency. Spray back of photograph with adhesive spray and attach to red cardstock.

Embellish photograph with photo corners and stickers as desired (photo A).

8. Using adhesive spray, attach photograph to transparency on back left side of coin holder. Embellish with rub-on letters and stickers (photo B).

9. Using adhesive spray, attach red cardstock to front of coin holder as desired. Using adhesive spray, adhere photographs to red cardstock, making sure to place photographs slightly askew so red cardstock shows behind. Embellish photographs as desired.

This container of memories was created using a recycled bottle and craft-store decorations.

Heritage Bottle

INSTRUCTIONS

1. Using masking tape, mask off top of bottle and 1" of neck.

2. Sand bottle to roughen surface, including bottom; wipe clean with soft cloth.

3. Spray two coats of primer on bottle including bottom; let dry after each coat.

4. Spray two coats of metallic spray paint on bottle including bottom and cork; let dry after each coat.

5. Spray two coats of satin finish on bottle including bottom; let dry after each coat. Remove masking tape.

6. Cut desired lace to fit around neck of bottle. Run thin bead of craft glue around neck along edge of metallic spray paint. Adhere lace around neck so it sits partially on unfinished glass; let dry.

7. Cut desired lace to fit around bottom of bottle. Run thin bead of craft glue around bottom of bottle and adhere lace to bottle; let dry.

8. Paint photo corners with leafing pen; let dry.

9. Spray photographs with digital photo and paper protectant spray; let dry. Place photo corners on corners of photograph. Adhere to bottle using craft glue; let dry. Add number stickers to photograph as shown (*photo A*).

10. Cut small photographs to fit charms. Adhere to charms using craft glue; let dry.

11. Add letter sticker to center of third charm.

12. Center and thread screw eye into top of cork.

13. Using needle-nose pliers, attach jump rings onto tops of charms. Attach jump rings onto one end of each piece of chain and attach to screw eye on top of cork. Determine desired length of chains and cut excess with wire cutters on pliers. Thread beads onto chains. Using pliers, attach frames to end of chains with jump rings.

14. Thread ribbon through screw eye so it is even on both sides; tie a half-knot.

15. Thread one end of ribbon through jump ring on one of remaining frames. Move frame to desired height; tie a half-knot.

16. Tie remaining frame to other side of ribbon.

Materials

- Beads: size and color of your choice (2)
- Charms: miniature frames (4)
- Cork stopper to fit bottle
- Craft glue
- Digital photo and paper protectant spray
- Glass bottle
- Jewelry chain: 2 strands, desired lengths and colors
- Jump rings: 4mm, color of your choice (7)
- Lace
- Leafing pen: silver
- Masking tape
- Metallic spray paint: sunset gold
- Needle-nose pliers with wire cutter
- Photo corners (4)
- Photograph: vintage, 2½"x 3½"
- Photographs: 2½"x 3½" (1); ½" round (2)
- Ribbon: ½" wide
- Sandpaper
- Satin finish spray
- Scissors
- Screw eye: small
- Soft cloth
- Spray primer: gray
- Stickers: letter, numbers

Sewing Frame

INSTRUCTIONS

1. Sand frame; wipe clean with soft cloth.

2. Spray two coats of primer on entire frame; let dry after each coat. After last coat is dry, sand smooth and wipe clean with soft cloth.

3. Spray two coats of interior-exterior spray paint on entire frame; let dry after each coat.

4. Spray three coats of iridescent spray paint on entire frame; let dry after each coat.

5. Spray two coats of satin finish on entire frame; let dry after each coat.

6. From sewing-themed scrapbook paper, cut ruler and words (*photo A*).

7. From ladies in hats scrapbook paper, cut three small heads and three large heads.

8. Lay frame flat. Using tweezers to hold images, spray back of ladies' heads, ruler, and words with adhesive spray. Adhere to frame as shown (*photo B*).

9. Place charms on frame as desired. Using pencil, mark placement of hole at top of each charm. Remove charms. Drill small hole at marks. Use hammer and miniature nails to adhere charms to frame.

10. Using craft glue, adhere rhinestones to frame as desired; let dry.

Materials

- Adhesive spray
- Charms: dresses (2), hanger (1)
- Craft glue
- Drill
- Drill bit: 1/16"
- Hammer
- Interior-exterior spray paint: ballet slipper
- Iridescent spray paint
- Nails: miniature
- Pencil
- Picture frame: 8" square with 3 1/8" square opening
- Rhinestones: small, assorted colors
- Sandpaper
- Satin finish spray
- Scissors
- Scrapbook paper: ladies in hats, sewing-themed
- Soft cloth
- Spray primer: white
- Tweezers

Celebrate the bonds of female friendship with the retro-inspired Sewing Frame.

123

Paper Finishes Colors

Krylon® Metallic

 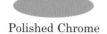 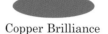

| 18KT. Gold Plate | Polished Chrome | Copper Brilliance |

Krylon® Stained Glass Sheer Color

| Blue | Red | Yellow | Green |

Krylon® Make It Stone!®

| Black Granite | White Onyx | Gold | Silver |

Krylon® Make It Suede!®

| Buckskin | Forest Glen |

Krylon® Glitter Spray

| Glistening Gold | Shimmering Silver |

Krylon® Webbing Spray

| Black Lava | White Whisper | Gold Chiffon | Silver Chiffon |

Krylon® Short Cuts® Paints

 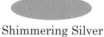   

Golf Leaf	Chrome	Red Pepper	Ocean Blue	Espresso	Sun Yellow	Muslin
Hot Pink	Burgundy	Leaf Green	Hunter Green	Glow Orange	Gloss White	Gloss Black
Flat White	Flat Black	Kiwi	Bonnet Blue	True Taupe	Forever Blue	Iris
Copper Kettle	Clear Gloss	Sand	Seashell	Cinnamon	Morning Mist	Antique Bronze
	Aquamarine	Turquoise	Tanzanite	Golden Pear	Celery	

Where to Find It

Krylon products are sold in art supply, crafts, and hardware stores.
To find a store near you, visit www.krylon.com.

Acknowledgements

**Red Lips 4 Courage
Communications, Inc.:**

Eileen Cannon Paulin,
Catherine Risling, Rebecca Ittner,
Jayne Cosh

8502 E. Chapman Ave. 303
Orange, CA 92869
www.redlips4courage.com

Book Editor: Rebecca Ittner

Copy Editor: Catherine Risling

Book Designer:
Kehoe+Kehoe Design Associates
Burlington, VT

Photo Stylist: Rebecca Ittner

Photographer:
Rick Szczechowski
Los Angeles, CA
www.etchlight.com

Designers:

Valoree Albert
Pages 26-27, 42-43

Madeline Arendt
Pages 70-71, 85-87

Stephanie Barnard
Pages 20-21, 23, 25

Lori Bergmann
Pages 18-19, 37, 67

Karen Blonigen
*Pages 82-84, 88-90, 95-98, 112-114,
116, 120-123*

Pam Canavan
Page 29

Madeline Fox
Pages 16-17

Colette George
Pages 108-111, 115-117, 124-127

Kris Gillespie
Pages 50-51

Barbara Housner
Pages 46-49

Eileen Hull
Page 73

Julie Johnson
Pages 30-31, 91, 105, 118-119

Lauren Johnston
Pages 36, 38-41

Becca Malone
Pages 22, 65

Jill Meyer
Pages 92-94

Roxi Phillips
Pages 52-59, 68-69, 72, 74-75, 78-81, 99-105

Aileen Roberts
Pages 62-64

Denise Tucker
Pages 34-35, 66

Sonia Viglianti
Pages 22, 24-25, 28

Janna Wilson
Pages 32-33

With special thanks to:

Sharon Currier

Currier Communications, Inc.
Chagrin Falls, OH
scurrier@curriercomm.com

Index

METRIC EQUIVALENCY CHARTS

inches to millimeters and centimeters (mm-millimeters, cm-centimeters)

inches	mm	cm	inches	cm	inches	cm
⅛	3	0.3	9	22.9	30	76.2
¼	6	0.6	10	25.4	31	78.7
½	13	1.3	12	30.5	33	83.8
⅝	16	1.6	13	33.0	34	86.4
¾	19	1.9	14	35.6	35	88.9
⅞	22	2.2	15	38.1	36	91.4
1	25	2.5	16	40.6	37	94.0
1¼	32	3.2	17	43.2	38	96.5
1½	38	3.8	18	45.7	39	99.1
1¾	44	4.4	19	48.3	40	101.6
2	51	5.1	20	50.8	41	104.1
2½	64	6.4	21	53.3	42	106.7
3	76	7.6	22	55.9	43	109.2
3½	89	8.9	23	58.4	44	111.8
4	102	10.2	24	61.0	45	114.3
4½	114	11.4	25	63.5	46	116.8
5	127	12.7	26	66.0	47	119.4
6	152	15.2	27	68.6	48	121.9
7	178	17.8	28	71.1	49	124.5
8	203	20.3	29	73.7	50	127.0

yards to meters

yards	meters	yards	meters	yards	meters	yards	meters	yards	meters
⅛	0.11	2⅛	1.94	4⅛	3.77	6⅛	5.60	8⅛	7.43
¼	0.23	2¼	2.06	4¼	3.89	6¼	5.72	8¼	7.54
⅜	0.34	2⅜	2.17	4⅜	4.00	6⅜	5.83	8⅜	7.66
½	0.46	2½	2.29	4½	4.11	6½	5.94	8½	7.77
⅝	0.57	2⅝	2.40	4⅝	4.23	6⅝	6.06	8⅝	7.89
¾	0.69	2¾	2.51	4¾	4.34	6¾	6.17	8¾	8.00
⅞	0.80	2⅞	2.63	4⅞	4.46	6⅞	6.29	8⅞	8.12
1	0.91	3	2.74	5	4.57	7	6.40	9	8.23
1⅛	1.03	3⅛	2.86	5⅛	4.69	7⅛	6.52	9⅛	8.34
1¼	1.14	3¼	2.97	5¼	4.80	7¼	6.63	9¼	8.46
1⅜	1.26	3⅜	3.09	5⅜	4.91	7⅜	6.74	9⅜	8.57
1½	1.37	3½	3.20	5½	5.03	7½	6.86	9½	8.69
1⅝	1.49	3⅝	3.31	5⅝	5.14	7⅝	6.97	9⅝	8.80
1¾	1.60	3¾	3.43	5¾	5.26	7¾	7.09	9¾	8.92
1⅞	1.71	3⅞	3.54	5⅞	5.37	7⅞	7.20	9⅞	9.03
2	1.83	4	3.66	6	5.49	8	7.32	10	9.14